D0152945

The Entrepreneur's Guide to Marketing

Recent Titles in
The Entrepreneur's Guide

The Entrepreneur's Guide to Managing Growth and Handling Crises
Theo J. van Dijk

The Entrepreneur's Guide to Writing Business Plans and Proposals
K. Dennis Chambers

The Entrepreneur's Guide to Hiring and Building the Team
Ken Tanner

The Entrepreneur's Guide to Managing Information Technology
CJ Rhoads

The Entrepreneur's Guide to Successful Leadership
Dan Goldberg and Don Martin

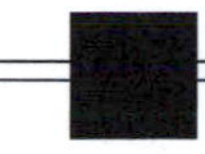

The Entrepreneur's Guide

CJ Rhoads, Series Editor

The Entrepreneur's Guide to Marketing

Robert F. Everett

PRAEGER

Westport, Connecticut
London

Library of Congress Cataloging-in-Publication Data

Everett, Robert F.
The entrepreneur's guide to marketing / Robert F. Everett.
p. cm. — (The entrepreneur's guide, ISSN 1939–2478)
Includes bibliographical references and index.
ISBN 978–0–313–35048–1 (alk. paper)
1. Marketing—Management. 2. Marketing—Decision making. 3. Small business marketing.
4. Sales management. I. Title.
HF5415.13.E896 2009
658.8—dc22 2008032608

British Library Cataloguing in Publication Data is available.

Library of Congress Catalog Card Number: 2008032608
ISBN: 978–0–313–35048–1
ISSN: 1939–2478

First published in 2009

Praeger Publishers, 88 Post Road West, Westport, CT 06881
An imprint of Greenwood Publishing Group, Inc.
www.praeger.com

Printed in the United States of America

The paper used in this book complies with the Permanent Paper Standard issued by the National Information Standards Organization (Z39.48–1984).

10 9 8 7 6 5 4 3 2 1

This book is dedicated to my father, Robert R. Everett, who taught me to always be curious and never accept the conventional wisdom; to my wife, Jan Orcutt, who provided many vital ideas and comments to this work; and to my daughter Morgan, who was born ''cable ready'' and remains my constant teacher.

Contents

Acknowledgments

This book involves ideas generated over thirty-five years of study, teaching, and consulting work. I would like to acknowledge the contributions of several key people in my development as a scholar and practitioner of business. These include my dissertation directors, Dr. Hart Nelsen and Dr. John McCarthy, formerly of Catholic University, now at Penn State University; Dr. Phil Kuehl and Dr. Tom Greer, formerly of the University of Maryland, who believed in me and gave me my first teaching job; and the hundreds of students I have had over the years who have challenged me and kept me young. On the practitioner side, I want to thank all of my clients over the years. I also want to acknowledge the late Al Boswell, who taught me much of what I know of diagnosing business problems. Finally, I would like to thank Dave Wimer of VR Marathon Business Group, Susan Milich of Federal Marketing Associates, and Dr. Larry Mazzeno, President Emeritus of Alvernia College for their ongoing encouragement and support of this work.

The preparation of this, my first book, would not have been possible without the support of my friend and colleague, C.J. Rhoads, the series editor, and Jeff Olson at Praeger Publishers, both of whom let me go through what it took to write this and made the whole process far easier and more rewarding than I ever expected.

Introduction

YOU ARE MUCH SMARTER THAN YOU THINK

You are reading this guide because you think you need help marketing your entrepreneurial product or service. You are right, but perhaps not in the way you think.

The fact that you are an entrepreneur, or are trying to be an entrepreneur, already says something about you. Although most people seem to be content (or discontented) to work their lives for someone else, you, for whatever reason, want to be your own boss. To me, that means you already know a great deal about the world and yourself. Although this is not the place to get into detail about the hundreds or thousands of various motivations people have for going into their own business, it is clear that you have your own, and they are important to you. The fact that you are an entrepreneur, or are trying to be an entrepreneur, also tells me that you already have the intelligence and the imagination to succeed. You just might not know it yet.

This book has been written based on a simple assumption:

You already know most of what you need to know to be successful at marketing. There are only three things you need to do:

1. Get rid of some of the habits of thought that are preventing you from using your substantial inborn intelligence.
2. Recognize that ideas and behaviors that you have learned in other places in your life are immediately relevant and applicable to marketing.
3. Learn the jargon associated with marketing so that you can talk to marketing people.

A Small Example

We've all heard the phrase, "Thinking outside the box." But do you know where the phrase comes from? There is a simple problem in creative thinking that I have seen in books and workshops many times over the years. It's called the "9 Dots Problem," and it looks like Figure I.1.

The goal is to connect all nine dots with four straight lines, but you cannot lift the pencil from the paper. Try it!

Some of you may have seen it right away, but most of you are having a problem. Are you doing the problem as shown in Figure I.2?

Are you drawing an imaginary box around the nine dots and then trying to stay inside that box with your four straight lines? If so you are:

1. Doing what almost everyone does, and
2. Unable to solve the problem.

Try getting rid of the "box" and allowing the lines to go outside of its boundaries. The solution is shown in Figure I.3.

Now that you know the answer, it seems pretty obvious, doesn't it? Then why do so many of us have problems solving problems? (I didn't get it the first time either.) There are a number of important reasons, but mostly it is because although we are plenty smart enough, we get in our own way.

Just for fun, can you connect all nine dots with one straight line?

How We Get in Our Own Way

Creativity is the sudden cessation of stupidity.

Edwin Land, Inventor of the Polaroid Camera

We Place Unnecessary Conditions on Problems

The 9 Dots Problem above is a clear example of how we place unnecessary conditions on our problems. Most people place the unnecessary condition that all four lines must fall inside the area formed by the nine dots. (Did we learn this in kindergarten when we were taught to color inside the lines?)

The concept of a "right answer" is ingrained in us in childhood. Our educational systems require us to ingest huge amounts of information (more and more every day). Test scores and grades are based on the extent to which our answers correspond with those predetermined by our teachers, the state, and/or the Educational Testing Service (SATs, etc.). Our ability to produce the "right" answer on demand determines our grades in school and can affect the colleges we can get admitted to, and even the jobs we can get. Believing the "right" things also affects our relationships, our job, our church, our political influence, and our prospects for the future.

I do not mean to imply that strongly held ideas and beliefs are wrong. Our beliefs and passions in large part make us who we are. But these beliefs can be limiting if they cause us to ignore or reject new or conflicting information or if they mean that we have a difficult time when confronted with new or difficult circumstances.

However, just because we are used to thinking in a certain manner does not mean that we are required to do so. Here are some suggestions:

Figure I.1
Nine Dots Problem

First, when faced with a problem or a situation you have never seen before, ask yourself: "What do I already believe or assume about this situation?" At first it will not be easy to identify everything you already believe, but you will surely be able to identify one or two preconceptions that you have.

It is important that you do not criticize yourself for having preconceptions. Preconceptions are a necessary part of operating in the world. And most of your preconceptions are probably right. All you need to do is notice as many of your preconceptions as you can. Then you can revisit these later if the problem seems difficult to solve. (Answer to the above problem: use a very wide line. I never specified the width the line had to be.)

Second, play with the situation. Make finding the solution fun. Sometimes you need to get outrageous. For example, in my New Product Management course, I have students pick an ordinary household product and try to find at least 100 new uses for it.

It Is Hard to Transfer Ideas and Lessons from One Area to Another

There is an old joke that goes: "There are two kinds of people in the world: those that sort things into two groups, and those that don't."

It is our natural tendency to sort ideas, situations, environments, people, and so on into groups. It is also our natural tendency to assume, incorrectly, that disparate groups have nothing in common. The structure of our

Figure I.2
Attempted Solution to 9 Dot Problem

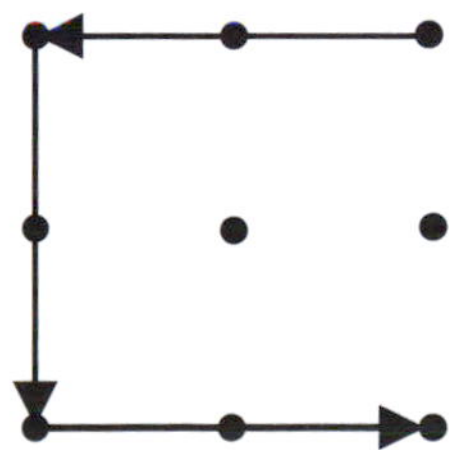

Figure I.3
Solution to 9 Dot Problem

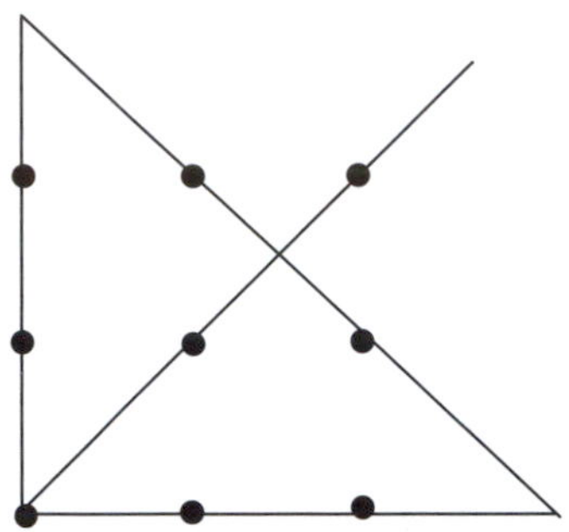

educational system tends to separate subject areas into nonoverlapping groups. Starting in junior high school, we get separate teachers for science, math, English, history, and so on. In high school, we get separate teachers for biology, chemistry, and physics. In college, we get separate teachers for biology, biochemistry, paleontology, zoology, botany, and in graduate school, the specializations can be mind boggling.

The same applies to business. We have specialists in general management, operations management, supply chain management, finance, international finance, accounting, mergers and acquisitions, marketing, new product development, business ethics, human resources, business strategy, and so on. Each of these specialties claims ownership of its own intellectual "turf." Each defines its own jargon, has its own consultants, and publishes its own books. It's no wonder that entrepreneurs like yourself might think that they need much more help than they do.

I'll try to cut through all this for you.

A core premise of this book is that the fundamental processes by which successful business relationships are created are the same as those by which personal relationships are created.

In other words, you do not have to learn about marketing from scratch when, in fact, you know at least 80 percent of what you need to know already! Feel better?

We Tend to Defer to "Experts"

Along with all of the separation of subject matter into distinct disciplines comes the proliferation of "experts."

There is good news and bad news about experts.

The good news is that experts stay current with the latest information in their fields. There is way too much information out there for any of us to comprehend. Experts are valuable for helping us sort through this vast array of knowledge to quickly find what we need. For example, all businesspeople should know a good lawyer and human resources consultant to help them comply with the federal, state, and local employment laws to which they are subject.

Professional experts also bring experience from other firms to their relationship with you. This experience can provide valuable insight and perspective in assessing and resolving your business issues.

Experts can lend credibility when you pitch your own ideas to banks, investors, employees, and partners. Experts can be valuable networking sources for customers, suppliers, investors, and others you may need.

The bad news is that experts can become too wedded to a particular approach or process, applying it to all clients regardless of specific circumstances.

Experts can become so deep in their own area of expertise they lose the ability to see situations involving more than their particular area. (There is an old adage: "To a man with a hammer, everything looks like a nail.") Experts may inappropriately think they know more about your business (or business in general) than you do.

Free Yourself

I want to be very clear here:

- Your beliefs are important.
- Organizing your life into manageable components is important.
- The separation of your business operations into reasonable functional components based on skills and expertise is important.
- Expert assistance is important.

My only point is that these factors should not be limiting. And it is the limits we place on our thinking, not our fundamental ability to think, that causes us difficulty.

Give yourself permission to "think outside of the box." Take what people say and use it as a starting point for your own thinking, not the ending point.

It is your business—your baby. In the end, your own imagination and common sense will be the keys to success.

OVERVIEW OF THIS BOOK

This book is all about how to figure things out for yourself. So, rather than give you some large buffet-like menu of techniques you might pick from, I am going to walk you through a careful process of

- Clarifying what you want
- Understanding your market and competition
- Understanding your own strengths and weaknesses

- Selecting the strategic approach you will take
- Choosing and implementing the best marketing techniques for you.

In Chapter 1, I present a unifying process for effective marketing that I have developed over close to 30 years of consulting and teaching experience. I then take you through that process, chapter by chapter.

Throughout the book I illustrate points in three ways:

1. Using examples from common products and services you are probably already familiar with
2. Providing anecdotal stories from my own professional experience to illustrate larger points
3. Utilizing a single entrepreneurial case to specifically illustrate the use of the tools presented in various chapters. This entrepreneur, Mike Jameson of Ted's Fish Market in the Boston area, is entirely fictitious. However, he serves as a unifying case so that you can follow the marketing process through from goal setting through implementation. This case will be described in much more detail at the end of Chapter 1.

1

Marketing Demystified

When you think of the word "Marketing," what pops into your head? Clever advertisements? Slogans? Junk mail?

Marketing has gotten a bad reputation over the years, primarily because of abuse by unthinking or unethical businesses. So let's start with what marketing is not.

Marketing is not about manipulating people. It is about influencing them. If marketers could actually manipulate people, we would all drive safely, buckle our seat belts, drink milk, and give generously to the college of our choice! We would get out and vote. It is precisely because marketing is usually not done well that people have to do so much of it.

MARKETING IS ALL ABOUT RELATIONSHIPS

Marketing is, in fact, a straightforward and essential part of every business. It is simply about creating and maintaining the relationships that an organization needs to operate. It is much more than just generating new customers. Marketing must also involve suppliers, competitors, partners, government, and the community at large. Marketing efforts must also include a company's employees and customers. In short, marketing is all about strong, reliable, and mutually profitable business relationships.

At their essence, business relationships are always personal. As soon as customers get close enough to an organization to deal with it, they are dealing with businesspeople, and those people bring to the business relationship all of their own goals, perceptions, experiences, biases, fears, moods, resentments, loyalties, and so on. Think about the relationships that you have had with business as a consumer and as a businessperson. Don't you experience the relationships with those businesses in terms of the people you deal with?

I would go so far as to argue that this same process extends to all social systems. In other words, the underlying process by which people interact with each other is the same as the process by which companies, nations, and even animals interact.

Here's the key point:

> If you have any successful relationships anywhere in your life with anyone (including your pet), then you already know how to market. You just need to learn how to apply that knowledge in a business setting.

THE RELATIONSHIP PROCESS

If marketing is all about relationships, then understanding the process of marketing requires understanding the process of relationships. So here goes.

To help my clients understand the process of marketing, I developed a model that one of my students (years ago) dubbed the "SPUR" (Strategic Process for Understanding Relationships). I will simply refer to it as the SPUR.

The SPUR consists of six questions and five actions. Although these are in a particular order for explanatory purposes, it does not mean that people go through these steps logically or in sequence. In general, we skip around in this model. We make tentative decisions about one part, then modify those decisions based on results or decisions about another part. Usually the whole process takes place outside of our conscious awareness. We "feel our way through."

There is nothing wrong with feeling our way through. It is the only way that works. At the same, time doing things consciously, rather than randomly, always works better in the long run.

The Six Core Questions

1. What do I want? At the core of any of our actions, including relationships, is our motivation. In a personal setting, what we want includes our long-term goals and aspirations as well as our more immediate needs and desires. In a business setting, these are the mission, goals, and nearer term objectives of our company.
2. *Who can give it to me?* If we were capable of meeting all of our needs by ourselves, we would not need others; but we can't, so we do. In a business sense, we need our suppliers, our investors, our employees, our advisors, our resellers, and, of course, our customers. The essential issue here is who we choose to develop a relationship with and are they actually capable of and willing to provide us with what we need.
3. *What do they want?* Relationships cannot work in the long run unless they are win—win. Both sides have to have some important needs met or the relationship ends. Entrepreneurs have to be especially careful here. It is extremely easy to think that people "should" want your product. However, perhaps the most important thing entrepreneurs

need to learn about marketing is that customers do not care what you think. They only care about what they think. Much of this book will be about helping you learn to think like a customer.

4. *What can I deliver?* This is another tough question. You cannot be all things to all people. You also have limited funds and limited operational capacity and time. You have to choose what you are going to be excellent at and focus on that that. This will require an honest and fearless assessment of your company, your products and services, and yourself.
5. *Who else can deliver it?* You have competition: Probably a lot more than you think. Knowing your competition and their strengths and weaknesses will help you find your own unique niche in the marketplace.
6. *What makes me special?* Customers are looking for something special. Entrepreneurs are looking to be special. Finding your place in the market, the place that customers see as uniquely and powerfully yours, can be one of the most exciting parts of the entire entrepreneurship process.

The Five Key Actions

1. *Offer what they want.* This is the step most people think of as marketing. This is the point at which you develop and communicate your message about what you have to offer. The most important thing here is that the messages you offer must be related to what the market wants, and given in the way the market wants to hear them.
2. *Ask for what you want.* Perhaps the biggest reason people do not get what they want in life is that they do not ask for it. If you have a good product that will provide significant benefit to your customer, ask a reasonable price (you're worth it) and ask the customer to buy (you'll be doing them a favor).
3. *Make a clear agreement.* Perhaps the biggest reason people become dissatisfied with relationships is disappointment, and disappointment is usually caused by inaccurate expectations. When we are trying to create relationships, personal or professional, it is all too easy to promise the world and figure that you'll straighten it all out later once you get the deal.
4. *Keep the agreement.* Broken promises are not acceptable in any relationship.
5. *Keep score.* If you are any good at what you do and feel any passion for your company and products, you are going to make mistakes. It's part of taking risks. If you are not willing to make mistakes, quit now and become an accountant.

But if you keep score—if you track what you are doing and fearlessly assess outcomes—you will continually learn from those mistakes and continually improve all aspects of your business.

HOW IT WORKS

Neither marketing nor the SPUR is a linear process. It is a much more circular (even spiral) process. Each step:

- Helps you focus more clearly on the step that follows, and
- Helps to clarify the steps that precede it.

In other words, rather than being a sequence of actions resulting in some conclusion, the SPUR is an ongoing process of focused inquiry, reflection, decision, action, assessment, and revision. An illustration of this can be seen in Figure 1.1.

This way of thinking should be continual. You are never done, but you keep getting closer to reaching your goals. Even when you are successful (as I expect you will be), your world will be constantly changing around you, and you will also have to change or be left behind.

Each of the six core questions in the SPUR may well provide you answers and insights that could cause you to revise conclusions and decisions you have already made.

Some examples:

- Your competitive analysis (Question 5) may show that what you thought was your most attractive target market (Question 2) is already saturated, but there is a somewhat less attractive market that looks like it could be all yours.
- You discover that certain features of your product (Question 4) are not as important to this new market (Question 3) as other features are. You reassess what makes you unique relative to this new market (Question 6).

Figure 1.1
Continual Thinking Illustration

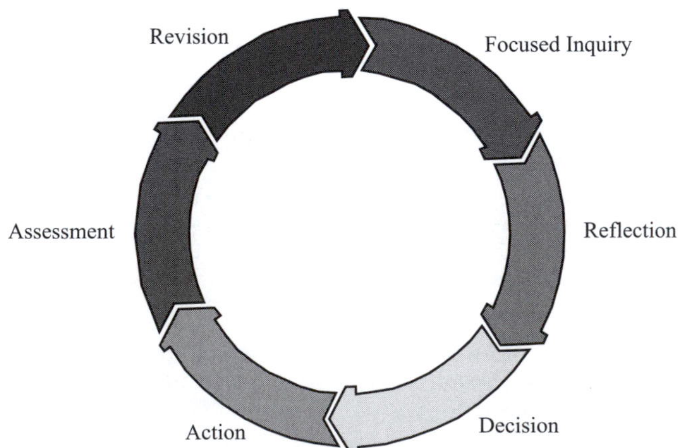

Seeking Alignment

A powerful way to think about this process is by striving for alignment. The answers to each of the six questions should fit together and not contradict the others. In other words:

1. Your goals (Question 1) should be realistic given your market (Question 2), your competitors (Question 5), your products and your resources (Question 4).
2. Your target market and business associates should be selected (Question 2) to best help you achieve your goals (Question 1).
3. You need to understand the needs of your target market and business associates (Question 3) and have the resources, products, and services (Question 4) to meet at least some of those needs.
4. Your products and services should offer a clear advantage (Question 6) over your competition (Question 5) in at least one area of importance (Question 3) to your target market (Question 2).

WHAT IS TO COME

The rest of the book will detail this approach. Each of the next fifteen chapters will explore steps in the SPUR in various ways. In addition to the conceptual discussion, each chapter will include stories, examples, practical exercises, worksheets, and suggestions for additional reading.

TED'S FISH MARKET: A CASE STUDY IN ENTREPRENEURIAL MARKETING

(Please note: This case is entirely fictional. There is no Ted's Fish Market in Boston or anywhere else I could find. If I have missed some real Ted's Fish Market anywhere, I wish you luck and would be delighted to send you a free copy of this book.)

Ted's Fish Market is a 100-year-old establishment near the center of Lexington, Massachusetts, a Boston suburb. Mike Jameson, the current owner of Ted's, took over the business from his father who purchased it about twenty-five years ago from the descendants of the original founders.

Ted's is a relatively small store (fewer than 2,000 square feet) located in a 200-year-old building that was once part of a farm. The store caters to locals, tourists, and commercial customers.

The fish and other seafood sold is purchased early each morning by Mike at a wholesale market in Gloucester and, whenever possible, directly from the fishermen. He prides himself on his skills in selecting the best products and negotiating good prices.

The store currently averages about $60,000 per month in sales of all types. Sales have been very steady for the last several years but growth in sales has been very slow, with a net increase of only 2 percent in the last two years.

Now that Mike has been running Ted's himself for more than a year, he feels that he is ready to kick-start growth by completely reassessing his marketing program. After careful consideration of several choices, Mike selected Praeger's *The Entrepreneur's Guide to Marketing* as his guide. He has committed himself to following each of the steps carefully to ensure the best results.

SUMMARY

☑ Marketing is all about relationships.

☑ When working on relationships, focus on what the other person wants and whether or not you can deliver it.

☑ The goal is to seek alignment between your capabilities and the other person's needs.

2

Marketing Applied: A Strategic Overview of Marketing

As an entrepreneur, you are most likely a person of action. Right now you have a great idea; maybe even a great product ready to be sold. You know that people would buy a lot from you if only they knew how fantastically, amazingly, mind-blowingly awesome your product or service is. And, right now, you are looking for a fast, powerful way to get that message out right now, but at a cost you can afford.

Ready, fire, aim! This can be a great strategy if you have the resources and time to make mistakes and learn from them before you go belly up. Not all entrepreneurs have that luxury.

TAKING A "STRATEGIC" APPROACH

On the chance that you are one of those entrepreneurs who has somewhat limited funds, it is essential that you think strategically. This means that before you jump in and attack your marketing, you first must spend a little time (how much depends on your own situation) thinking through what you are going to do.

As I discussed in the last chapter, marketing is a relationship process. You must have good answers (or at least progress toward good answers) to the Six Core Questions before you start spending your valuable, scarce capital on marketing actions that could have a significant chance of failure.

The Covey Matrix

In his classic book, *The 7 Habits of Highly Effective People*, Dr. Stephen Covey provides a wonderfully simple, two-dimensional chart of tasks. I have adapted this chart for our purposes in Figure 2.1.

Covey points out that some tasks are important while others are not very important. At the same time, some tasks appear to be urgent while others are not urgent.

Figure 2.1
An Adaptation of Covey's Matrix

Types of Tasks	Urgent	Not Urgent
Important	Crises	Effectiveness
Not Important	Distractors	Wasted Effort

For you, the entrepreneur, some examples of these are:

Urgent and Important

- Customer delivery deadlines
- Customer support
- Payroll
- Accounts payable

Urgent, but Not Important

- Some phone calls
- Some meetings
- Some email

Not Urgent, but Important

- Business planning
- Marketing planning
- New product development
- Calling current customers
- Recreation and skill development

Not Urgent and Not Important

- Busy work
- Straightening up the office
- Some phone calls, meetings, and email

Covey's main insight, however, is in noting that once we take care of our crises (the urgent, important tasks), most people then go on to deal with the urgent, not important tasks. The result is that little if any time is left over for the important, but not urgent tasks, and it is these activities that most determine success or failure.

Other Reasons Entrepreneurs Don't Plan

Strategic planning is one of the most important of these nonurgent tasks. However, because it is not urgent (and appears difficult), planning is one of the first things to get set aside by entrepreneurs.

There are a few other, similarly wrong ideas that can get in the way of a good planning effort. These include:

- *Laziness*: You have a lot to do as an entrepreneur. You don't think you should need to do one more thing. Besides, you've never done this before, and it's better to have no plan at all than to have a poor one.
- *Overconfidence/Hubris*: You are a really smart person with a really great product. All you need to do is get going, and you will be able to figure it all out later.
- *Fear of failure or the unknown*: Planning requires a searching and fearless evaluation of your market, your competition, your product, and yourself. That can be pretty scary.
- *Expense*: Because you don't know how to do an excellent planning effort, you will need to hire a consultant and can't afford one.
- *Previous bad experience*: You planned once before and things didn't turn out as you planned. So this time you won't bother.

Ask yourself honestly if any (or all) of the above thoughts have occurred to you. If so, don't worry; they occur to everyone.

Why You Should Plan

There are five compelling reasons why you should plan your marketing efforts.

1. *Finite resources:* You only have so much money and so much time. I am guessing that you do not have enough of either to go about wasting them. Although a good plan will neither guarantee success nor ensure that no time or resources are wasted, it will greatly reduce the likelihood and scope of waste.
2. *Uncertainty about competitive strengths*: It is all well and good to be proud of your accomplishments so far and confident of your success. Just remember that your competition feels just as proud and confident, and your market doesn't care whether you are proud or confident. The marketplace cares whether you will do a better job for it than your competition does. It is imperative that you know where you stand. By the way, if you know what you are doing, your analysis will lead to a justifiable increase in your confidence.
3. *Irreversible commitment of resources*: There is an old Buddhist saying: "You cannot cross a chasm in two leaps." In other words, if you want you marketing (or anything else) to be effective, you must decide what to do, then make the commitment necessary to do it right. If you hold back because you are afraid to be wrong or because you want to hedge your bet, you are inviting failure. It is much better to invest a little time in scoping things out first, then commit.
4. *Need to get all aspects of the company to work together*: Finally, it is important to get everyone in your organization and everyone working with

your organization (e.g., suppliers, bankers, partners, customers) telling the same story about who you are and what you do.

5. *Need to know what to change if things are not working*: If you have gone through the planning process, you have developed a sense of what you are and are not sure of regarding the facts and assumptions upon which your plan is based. Then, if things are not working the way you expected, you know exactly where to look to make revisions.

The Bottom Line

In the end, you really only have one choice:

- Plan—and make success up to you, or
- Don't plan—and leave success up to chance.

THE STRATEGIC PROCESS

So, at this point we know we should think strategically and that all kinds of potential disasters could befall you and your firm if you don't. It is now a good time to ask, "What does a marketing strategy look like?"

Marketing strategy can be distilled down to two critical questions:

1. Who are my best potential customers?
2. In what way can I be seen by them as special?

These are never easy questions to answer. They require thoughtful (but not necessarily very time-consuming) research and analysis.

Your Best Customers

It is usually easy to look out into the marketplace and identify the largest demographic group you can that might be interested in what you have and decide that they are your target market. Then all you need to do is come up with a powerful promotion program that convinces them to abandon buying from your competition, or whatever else they were doing, and buy from you. Wrong!

This is like a run straight up the middle in football. If you are strong enough and hardy enough, you can eke out yard after yard and, perhaps, prevail. But the cost can be high, and victory is not ensured. Better to utilize the wide receiver out in the open, undefended, who could run for the touchdown, making the defenders irrelevant.

In other words, as a new business, your best customers will be those that are unserved or underserved by your competition and, among whom, you can establish a firm market position. In marketing, this is known as "targeting."

This usually means that you find and focus upon the biggest pond in which you can be the biggest fish. As your business, reputation, skills, and

financial resources grow, you can always make the pond larger or even expand into other ponds. For right now, however, play the game you can win.

Being Seen as Special

One way of looking at targeting is to ask, "How would I like to be seen as special?" Then look for those parts of the overall marketplace that would be most likely to appreciate that unique quality. For example:

- Low-cost provider: If your product or service meets the general needs of customers, but can do so at a price lower than that of your primary competitors, you may want to target customers likely to be price sensitive. Targets could include young families, the elderly, students, immigrants, and the generally less affluent. Examples of firms that use this strategy include Wal-Mart, Costco, Southwest Airlines, McDonalds, Hyundai, and the "house brands" offered by such stores as CVS and Walgreens.
- Differentiating features or values. Perhaps what makes you special is not pricing, but some other powerful aspect of your product. You would then target people who would appreciate that particular aspect. For example:
    - Mercedes: People who appreciate luxury and state-of-the-art engineering
    - BMW: People who like prestige and the "ultimate driving experience"
    - Volvo: People whose primary consideration is safety
    - Chevrolet: People who desire to buy American cars
    - Jeep: People who want rugged vehicles
- Market niche specialization. It is not necessary to pick just one target market. There may be many specific, but related needs that the market has that you can fill with a line of related products. Tylenol is a good example here. Johnson & Johnson offers the following versions of Tylenol, each for people with specific pain relief needs:
    - Regular Strength
    - 8 Hour
    - Menstrual Relief
    - Arthritis
    - Allergy Multisymptom
    - Allergy Multisymptom Night Time
    - Severe Allergy
    - Sinus Congestion & Severe Pain
    - and 28 others
- Specialized operational expertise. A related approach is to present yourself as the expert in a particular operational area. This is the common practice among doctors (general practitioner, ophthalmologist, oncologist, psychiatrist, etc.), lawyers (corporate law, tax law, business law, criminal defense, etc.), and college professors (medieval history, British literature, marketing, etc.) Each specialty evolves from a specific market need.

In marketing, your uniqueness in the marketplace relative to your competitors is known as your "market position." This is discussed extensively in Chapter 6.

KEY STEPS IN STRATEGIC PLANNING

There are six main steps in the strategic planning process. As we see, these correspond closely to the eleven steps of the relationship model discussed in the previous chapter.

These six steps are:

- Define goals
- Assess environment
- Develop strategy
- Identify tactics
- Implement
- Measure and revise

I will go over each in turn.

Step 1: Define Goals

There is an old Chinese saying: "If you do not know where you are going, any road will take you there." The most critical part of developing any strategy is being clear about what you want to accomplish. Chapter 3 is all about this.

Step 2: Assess Environment

The next most important question is, "What is going on here?"

The answer to this question requires a careful scoping out and evaluation of the total environment in which you operate. That includes your external environment and your internal environment.

The External Environment

Your external business environment consists of:

- Your customers
- Your marketplace
- Your partners
- Your suppliers
- Your distributors/outlets
- Your competitors
- Your bank
- The government (national and local)
- The communities in which you operate
- Perhaps a trade or professional association
- Perhaps a labor union
- And, any individual or organization that is affected in any way by what you do (These are often called "stakeholders").

This is the part of the environment you cannot control. However, you can influence any and all parts of this external environment. Influencing the external environment is the purpose of marketing.

Aspects of your environment can be put into four broad categories:

1. *Opportunities:* Opportunities are aspects of your external environment that you can potentially take advantage of to meet your business goals. Examples include:
   - Unmet market demand for a product or service you can or could provide
   - Growth in key market segments
   - Success of channel partner who is selling your products
   - Increased demand for your product type
   - Decline/demise of key competitor
   - Positive change in regulatory environment
2. *Threats:* A threat is some aspect of your external environment that could adversely affect your business. For example:
   - Competitive introduction of new technology
   - Lower-priced entry in the market
   - Well-funded entry in the market
   - Declining market size
   - Regulatory attack
   - Union problems
3. *Operational issues:* Operational issues are neither opportunities nor threats, but simply things you must take care of. Government regulations usually fit in here. For example, you need to file your taxes, pay your landlord, and comply with environmental and OSHA regulations. However, not taking care of these issues can create a threat (e.g., the IRS coming after you).
4. *Irrelevancies:* These are the parts of the business environment that you can safely disregard when developing your marketing program. For instance, a competitor may introduce a product in a market that you do not plan to operate in.

The Internal Environment

Your internal environment is that part of your total business environment that you can control. Examples are:

- Products
- New product development
- Manufacturing
- Distribution
- Management
- Employee selection
- Finance
- Accounting

- Marketing
- Customer service
- Partner/supplier selection and service.

A note of caution here: When considering what is internal, the issue is not whether that function is, in fact, a part of or owned by your company. If you have operational control of resources provided by someone else (e.g., contract manufacturing, shipping, temporary help), then those resources are considered to be internal.

Putting External and Internal Together

The SWOT Analysis. A SWOT Analysis covers strengths, weaknesses, opportunities, and threats. When I present SWOT Analysis to my clients or my students, I use the diagram in Figure 2.2.

Figure 2.2
SWOT Analysis

	Inside	Outside
Good News	Strengths	Opportunities
Bad News	Weaknesses	Threats

Ted's Fish Market Example: To provide an example, here is a simple SWOT Analysis for Ted's Fish Market, the fictional New England emporium.

Strengths

- Freshest possible fish
- Reasonable prices
- Friendly service
- Excellent local reputation
- Large group of regular, loyal customers
- 100 years old
- Excellent location
- Historic building

Weaknesses

- Not well known outside of the local area
- Limited types of fish
- Relatively small facility, limiting growth
- Limited financial resources

Opportunities

- Increasing number of tourists coming to the area
- U.S. government says per capita consumption of fish is increasing

- Boutique food stores becoming popular
- Boston suburbs remain economically healthy
- Upscale people moving into other parts of the area to take advantage of lower housing prices

Threats

- Wholesale prices for fish are increasing
- Increasing dependency of foreign fisheries
- Weather and global warming
- Potential for increased government regulation

Recommendations Regarding SWOT Analysis

Key Point #1: The purpose of a SWOT Analysis is not to come to conclusions. The purpose of a SWOT Analysis is to make sure you ask all the right questions.

My experience is that once you get good answers to the right questions, the path to success becomes much more obvious.

When doing a SWOT Analysis, I recommend that you take these steps: First, do a "mind dump." This is like a one-person brainstorming session. Jot down everything and anything you can think of that might possibly have anything to do with your business. Walk through each of the external and internal factors mentioned above. Keep this as an ongoing list. Edit it as you learn more.

Next, ask as many people as you can to add information, perspectives, and insights. Focus on your partners, employees, and customers. Insist on the truth! Bad news may sting a bit, but it will hurt nowhere near as much as a bad marketing program will.

Now, go through your list (you can do this at any time and as often as you like) and ask the following three questions about each statement:

- Is this information relevant? Does this information make any real difference to me or my business? If it does not make a difference right now, ask yourself if it might make a difference in the future or if current circumstances change.
- If the information makes no difference at all, eliminate it from your list. The goal here is to drill down to the main factors to be considered in your marketing strategy.
- If the information or issue might make a difference in the future, you can still take it out of the current SWOT, but note it as something you need to keep your eye on.
- Is this information objective? Is it based on fact or judgment? There is nothing wrong with putting the judgments of yourself or others into your SWOT Analysis. However, it is critical that you make the distinction between fact and judgment.
- Is this information reliable? What is the evidence? Is my source credible? I have found in my consulting experience than even the most ethical, well intentioned business owners and managers will have

misconceptions and biases, especially when it comes to their own business. After all, your business is one of your most precious achievements.

Key Point #2: Your SWOT Analysis is an ongoing project. It is not a one-time event. Your internal and external environments are constantly changing. As your SWOT evolves, it can serve as a guide for tracking those environmental changes.

Step 3: Develop Your Strategy

With a good SWOT Analysis firmly in hand, you can now begin the process of developing a powerful and effective marketing strategy and clearly defining your target market and the market position you would like to hold in it.

When making these decisions, it is important to look at the total picture at each point. For example, suppose you make uniquely designed furniture. Furniture is a very crowded and competitive marketplace. There are some very high-end manufacturers and some very inexpensive manufacturers (e.g., Ikea). And these compete with an active used and antique furniture market. Your choice of a target market will depend simultaneously on at a minimum:

- Your own uniqueness
- What your pricing has to be to make a profit
- What other companies are offering products that may be perceived by the marketplace as similar to yours
- What resources you have to invest in penetrating that market.

In other words, you will need to look at your whole SWOT Analysis in one glance to see how all of the facts and opinions you have gathered will come together to form a single picture.

Fortunately, there is an analytical tool you can use to do this. It is called the "SWOT/TOWS" Analysis.

The SWOT/TOWS Analysis combines strengths, weaknesses, opportunities, and threats in an action-based format. It looks like Figure 2.3.

Figure 2.3
SWOT/TOWS Analysis

	Strengths	Weaknesses
Opportunities	Take Advantage	Build
Threats	Defend	Avoid

Putting the results of your SWOT Analysis into this context generates four important questions:

1. How can I best use my strengths to take advantage of my opportunities?
2. What capabilities do I need to build?
3. How do I best use my strengths to defend against the threats my business faces?
4. What threats must be avoided?

Step 4: Identify Tactics

Once your strategy is clearly defined, developing your implementation plan becomes largely a matter of the time and resources you are willing and able to invest in it.

In Chapter 8, I discuss some of the many tactical options you may have open to you.

Step 5: Implement

This is where you actually do, rather than just plan.

Step 6: Measure and Revise

This is where you keep yourself on track by carefully measuring results and reassessing your actions.

CONCLUSION: WHAT IS A GOOD STRATEGY?

- Clear definition of goals and acceptable means
- Match between needs of market and corporate strengths
- Provides a clear differential advantage over competition in one or more target market segments
- Is attainable without undue risk, financial or other, on the company
- Is perceived as clear and worthwhile to employees
- Is perceived as sensible to investors and other stakeholders.

SUMMARY

☑ Always take a strategic approach to marketing.
☑ Focus on the important, rather than urgent, tasks.
☑ Planning is critical for success.
☑ The best customers are those that are unserved or underserved by your competition.
☑ It is essential to be seen as special.
☑ There are six steps to strategic planning.
☑ SWOT Analysis can be very useful.

3

What Do I Want?

When planning the marketing for your business, it is essential that you have an extremely clear idea of the goals for yourself and for your business.

My first real experience as a consultant almost made me quit the business. After I started my teaching career, I started doing small business consulting to supplement my income. One of my first clients was Rick, the owner of a small (< $2 million) local manufacturer/retailer of home entertainment products who asked me to make some recommendations to improve his marketing program. A review of the company's program quickly showed that he was spending over $250,000 per year on ads in major national magazines. I went in to see Rick to review my initial findings. The last part of the conversation went like this:

Bob: Are you aware that you are spending over a quarter of a million dollars on magazine ads?

Rick: Of course.

Bob: (Hoping to find a reason other than insanity) Are you getting any response from these ads?

Rick: Of course! (And he proudly produced from beneath his desk a cardboard box about three inches deep in business reply cards.)

Bob: But are you making any sales off these leads?

Rick: Of course! I sold over $75,000 in product last year.

Bob: That's not much of a return. Don't you think you should cut out spending all that money?

Rick: No way!!! I need to prepare the marketplace for when we go into national distribution.

Bob: (Thinking maybe he wasn't crazy after all) So how long have you been doing this?

Rick: (Casually) Oh, about seven years.

My head was spinning. I stalled for time. "Let's have lunch tomorrow and talk more," I said, and left.

On the drive home I felt frustrated and furious (and fantasized about the award-winning campaign I could launch with $250,000). How could I help someone who wouldn't listen, who was wasting money, who was an idiot!?! Why was I doing this stupid consulting when I could quit starving as a college professor and get a real job? As these thoughts occupied my mind, the memory of something a successful consultant friend of mine once said emerged: "People almost never tell you the truth about what they really want. Because they almost never tell themselves the truth about what they really want."

I thought, "Maybe there is something going on here I just don't understand," and resolved to find out.

The next day at lunch an idea occurred to me. "Tell me the story of your life," I asked him after we had settled in a quiet booth. He took a deep breath, opened his mouth, and talked for three straight hours! Of that time, two hours were spent relating tales of a two-year period while he was in his late twenties (he was over fifty at the time we were talking). During that two-year period, he was national sales manager for a major national electronics company.

And the truth slowly dawned on me. If being sales manager of a national company in his twenties was so very important to him, might being president of a national company in his fifties also be very important to him? Despite the fact that almost all of his business was local, by buying all of the national magazine advertising he could afford, he could maintain that he was, in fact, the president of a national company. No wonder he would not hear of cutting out that effort. My anger and frustration was replaced with understanding. I knew what his real goal was.

From then on it was easy. I suggested developing a more effective response procedure to turn whatever leads he received into more sales. I also suggested a sales tracking system to identify exactly where his leads and sales were coming from. He loved it. Over time, sales increased. He paid more attention (and money) to those sources that were producing the most results, and some of the excess advertising was curtailed. Perhaps the national advertising effort remained a money loser, but it was less of one. We both felt like our relationship had been successful.

DEFINING GOALS

As the story illustrates, goals are not simple things. Yet goals are an essential part of our experience as human beings. It is our wants, our needs, our desires that motivate us to action, that direct the actions we take, and that often produce our judgments about ourselves and others.

This chapter looks at the nature of wants and how we can identify and clarify what our real motivations are: personal and professional.

WHAT IS A WANT?

The concept "want" is surprisingly difficult to define. Dictionary definitions are either circular (defining want as "need" or "desire") or negative (defining want in terms of "lack"). Yet we all experience many of our wants as very positive, beneficial, or even altruistic. Rather than get into an academic/philosophical/psychological discussion of what the correct definition of "want" might be, I would prefer to look at "want" in terms of our experience of it.

We "want" something when we think that our life, or the life of someone we care about, would be better if only we/they had/could/did X. Where "X" is the thing we want to have, do, or be.

There are two words in this definition which are critical: "think" and "better." Wants are based on perceptions and judgments. To want something, we must first perceive that we do not already have it. If we do not know about something, we cannot want it. If we already have it, strictly speaking we cannot also want it. We may want to keep it or want more of it, but those again imply something about the future, and we never "have" the future.

We must also believe that we would be better off if we did have it. This means that some criteria must exist so that we know what "better" means. The implication of this definition, then, is that unless you understand your own perceptions and judgments, you can't understand what it is you want.

On the other hand, we still want things, even when we do not understand why. In these circumstances, we experience our wants in terms of the emotional reaction and/or the motivation that we get from imagining having something we do not now have.

UNDERSTANDING MORE ABOUT WHAT I WANT

The goal-framing process is where we start to understand our wants.

Tool 3-A: The Goal-Framing Process

Because wants are complex and involve perceptions and judgments, it is important to look at the various aspects of each want you may have if you are to more fully understand it. I use the following five steps:

1. What do I want?
2. How will I know I have it?
3. What will it mean to me to have it?
4. What will get in my way?
5. What will I commit to in order to get it?

These five steps are frequently used by experienced consultants and workshop facilitators to arrive at a group consensus regarding a task or process to be accomplished. I also apply these steps with myself and other individuals to determine and clarify personal and organizational goals. I take these five steps one at a time, using personal and business examples.

What Do I Want?

This is the initial statement of a goal or the goal as we usually think about it. For example:

- I want a $100,000/year income.
- I want my children to have a good education.
- I want to increase my profits.
- I want to grow by 15 percent per year.
- I want to be the premier company in my industry.

How Will I Know I Have It?

In this step you define the criteria by which you will evaluate your success in achieving the goal.

Using education as an example, how would you define a "good education"? For some that may mean an Ivy League undergraduate degree followed by a graduate degree at a top university for that field. For others, it may mean finishing college or even high school. For others, it may mean that their children should attend the same college that they did. Or it may relate to grades, or fields of study, or any of a number of other criteria.

Chances are that if it is your goal, you have some idea, maybe just an unconscious idea, as to what you are really talking about when you say "good education." At the same time, by articulating those criteria, even to yourself, you will greatly improve your motivation and direction toward achieving that goal. And the more detailed and specific you are, the more motivated you will feel.

Take a moment right now and try it on some goal or want that you experience. Close your eyes and ask yourself the question: "If I opened my eyes right now and I had what I wanted, what would I see? What would I know? What would be different?" Try to be as clear, specific, and detailed as possible. If you come up with something interesting, you may want to write it down.

Notice how you feel. Are you more motivated or less motivated? Does the goal seem more real or more like a fantasy? Can you start to see some of the steps that will lead you to your goal? Keep practicing on the various wants, needs, and goals that you imagine you have. The more you practice, the better it works.

Now, let's take a business example. I commonly hear small business owners say that they want to increase their profitability. But what do they really mean?

First of all, what do they mean by profit? Is it

- Gross margin?
- Operating profit?
- Taxable profit?
- Net profit after taxes and depreciation?
- Measured in percentage?
- Measured in total dollars?

These can yield very different, even contradictory numbers. Or by "increasing profit" do they really mean

- Raising prices?
- Increasing sales?
- Cutting costs?
- Eliminating certain products/services?

Again, the choice here is critical.

And once you choose the parameters against which you will measure your success, you then need to decide how much and by when. A well-formed profit goal would then look like this:

"My goal is to increase my net dollar profit by 18 percent over the next twelve months."

What Will It Mean to Me to Have It?

This step looks at the importance of your goal, the value that you place on it. Is this goal critical to financial survival, self-esteem, or some other aspect of personal/family health or welfare? In other words, do you experience the goal as something you must have or is it simply something you would like to have?

What usually happens is that when people start looking closely at what a particular goal means to them, they become aware that their goal is really tied to some other, deeper, more emotional goal, like in the story that started this chapter. I may want a Mercedes because I want to impress my neighbors or clients, or because my father drove one and I want to feel equal to him, or because I think women will like it, or because one of my children was injured in a car accident and I think Mercedes are extremely safe. Goals may even (often) be nested three or four levels deep and/or may relate to several deeper needs. I want the $100,000 income so I can save a lot of money and so I can buy all the things I want my children to have. I want to save money so that my family will be secure. I want to save money so that I feel secure if something happens to me. I want my children to have all the good things I never had (or did have).

Close your eyes again and recall the goal you thought about before. Only this time examine your feelings about the goal. How important is this goal to you or to someone you love? Is this something you want because it will help you get to something even bigger? How will you feel about yourself and you life if you get this?

Now go back to the business example from before. Why would you want to increase profits? (This question is more important than it seems. It is your motivation toward this goal that will be the greatest determinant of success.)

- More personal income?
- Investment in growth?
- New product development?
- Product enhancement?
- Environmental change?
- Competitive pressure?

Again, each of these may suggest a different level of need and a different approach to goal achievement.

In addition, each of these may suggest a new set of goals. For example, if I am interested in increasing profits because I really want to get additional money to finance new product development, I have to ask myself why I want the new product. If it is to create more profit, am I in a chicken-and-egg situation? In my experience, most business leaders have these unexamined, unclarified goals. Fortunately, in my experience, these goals do get resolved when they are examined carefully.

What Will Get in My Way?

This is where it starts to get really interesting. Examining the practicality of our wants and goals is something that many people do not do and, in fact, may avoid doing.

Practicality can be looked at from two vantage points. The first is internal: How will I sabotage myself, that is, get in my own way? The second is external: What external circumstances could prevent me from getting what I want? It is important that both be examined. Sometimes we are inclined to blame the outside world for things that we are responsible for ourselves and sometimes we blame ourselves for things we have no control over. If we are unwilling to be ruthlessly honest with ourselves and with our environment, we have set up one more barrier to the achievement of our goal.

There are always internal and external hurdles to accomplishing any goal. The key is in recognizing what we can and cannot control. Look at Figure 3.1.

Even if we have an accurate view of the external obstacles that we face in reaching our goal, we can still sabotage ourselves by:

- Stressing out over things we cannot control.
- Avoiding (consciously or unconsciously) taking responsibility for things that we can, in fact, control.

This concept is best summarized by the famous Serenity Prayer:

God, Grant me the Serenity to accept the things I cannot change,
The Courage to change the things I can,
And the Wisdom to know the difference.

Figure 3.1
Responsibility vs. Control

		Can I Control This? Yes	Can I Control This? No
Do I feel responsible for this?	Yes	Power	Stress
	No	Avoidance	Acceptance

Most people have mixed feelings about almost everything they want. Goals may appear to conflict or require trade-offs: for example, you may want to provide the best of everything for your family and want to save money for your retirement. You may believe that the goal is impossible, for example, too much competition, poor economy, and so on. You may feel inadequate, unworthy, overwhelmed, or hold any number of other negative beliefs that get in your way of reaching that goal. You may be prone to procrastination, overcommitment, or any of a number of other behaviors that inhibit your ability to reach your goal.

It is important to recognize that goals do not exist in a vacuum. There will always be ideas, beliefs, and other goals that may conflict with, inhibit, or otherwise interfere with what you want to do.

At the same time, there are also likely to be barriers over which we have no control. Many "motivational" speakers and self-help books will try to convince you that there is nothing that you cannot accomplish if you so choose. And that may be true if you choose only one goal and spend all of your energy achieving it.

But most of us lead more complicated lives and experience many dreams and have many responsibilities that we choose not to abandon in search of some single Holy Grail. For us, it is important to clearly assess the constraints that our life has placed on us (or that we have chosen to place on ourselves) to assess the actual time, energy, emotional effort, and money that we would have to invest in this goal.

Close your eyes and think once again about the goal with which you have been working. Are your thoughts and feeling about this goal consistent? Do you have doubts about whether the goal is worth the effort or about whether you deserve to have it? Play devil's advocate for a moment. Who or what could get in your way? Your spouse? Family member? Colleague? The government? Some enemy of yours? Allow yourself to be truly honest in this evaluation. Are you feeling excited? Frustrated?

Back to the business example. What would be some of the constraints to increasing profits? It obviously depends on the strategy you plan to use. Suppose the strategy is cutting costs while maintaining competitive pricing. Any of the following could get in the way of this strategy being successful:

- Increased competitive price pressure
- Long-term contracts with important customers
- Labor contracts
- Increasing energy prices or other uncontrollable external forces
- Loyalty to workers
- Commitment to a particular location
- Reluctance to outsource off-shore

What Will I Commit to, to Get It?

This is the point at which you look at what you really have to do to achieve your goal. By now you know what the goal is, what achievement of the goal will mean to you, and what barriers may exist to that achievement. Getting what you want requires a commitment. You must spend the time, the energy, the money, the emotion, or whatever it takes if that goal is to be achieved.

As you honestly examine what that will take, it may turn out that you have underestimated the investment necessary. In that case you may want to reexamine that goal in that light. Or, what is often the case, you may have overestimated what it will take and thereby begin to experience your goal as more of a possibility. Now your motivation will increase, your pleasure in approaching the task will increase, and your likelihood of achieving your goal will greatly increase.

Close your eyes one last time and try this out on your goal. Imagine that you are actually doing what you need to do to reach that goal. Is it easier or harder than you imagined? Are there resources or assistance that you have that you did not think of before? How motivated do you feel? Are you enjoying this?

If, in doing this exercise over these steps, you have found yourself getting more excited, more motivated, and happier about your goal, then you have taken a major step toward getting what you want. If, on the other hand, you find yourself feeling frustrated, depressed, or angry while doing this exercise, you may want to think about whether that goal is really what you want for yourself. In general, the closer we get to what we want, the better we feel.

Ted's Fish Market Example

When Mike Jameson of Ted's Fish Market went through this process, he came up with the following, well formulated business goal:

What do I want?

- A 100-percent increase in gross revenue over the next 24 months.

How will I know I have it?

- Top line revenue will meet my goal.
- Net profit will at least double.
- Growth will be through sales, not acquisition.

What will it mean to me to have it?

- I will be closer to my dream of Ted's being the premier fish market in the Boston area.
- My future, and that of my family, will be more secure as my business becomes more valuable.
- Profits will increase as costs drop when I am able to buy fish in much larger quantities.

What will get in my way?

- Financial pressure from banks for near-term profits.
- The difficulty of obtaining loans I will need.
- Family pressure not to work any harder than I am now.
- Pressure from my father who wants things to remain as they were when he was running the business.

What will I commit to in order to get it?

- An increase in my personal workload.
- A moderate increase in business risk.
- Increased delegation of operations as I focus on growth.
- Maintaining a happy and healthy family life.

Cost–Benefit Analysis

In business, we often call this five-step process a "cost–benefit analysis." In a cost–benefit analysis, the business executive tries to make a careful assessment of:

- The goal
- The way success will be measured
- The expected benefits of achieving that goal
- The risks that must be taken
- The costs of the various activities required.

(Note how these five steps mirror the five steps of the goal-framing process.)

Putting them all together, the executive can assess the level of investment that must be made to reach the goal. The choice can then be made as to whether or not that goal is worth pursuing or whether the same time and resources could better be spent elsewhere.

Discussions of cost–benefit analysis, as well as the procedures for it, can be found in almost any introductory textbook on finance. There are also many trade books available in your local bookstore that will describe how to do this analysis.

However, it has been my experience that the fundamental clarification of goals, as discussed in this chapter, is best done without resorting to a formalized process. It is best when you "own" your own goals and the process by which you developed them. Using a formal process often results in a certain level of detachment from the results, and that is the last thing you need right now.

Understanding Business Goals

Clarifying goals becomes even more difficult in business, because personal and organizational goals are usually intertwined. In addition, there is usually an unspoken assumption that personal goals must be subordinated to organizational goals.

But in the real world this is almost never the case. People who own or work for organizations are people first and entrepreneurs/employees second. Personal needs and agendas will always affect organizational behavior and performance. Our only choice is whether we are going to be honest and open about it or we are going to ignore it.

In my years of experience as a consultant, I have found that the single most important issue in establishing any kind of organizational program or policy is determining the impact that it will have on the people who own or work for that organization.

Revenue, profit, market share, reputation, awards, growth rates, or any other "business" goals are, in the final analysis, meaningless. They are only a means (or a barrier) to the achievement of the personal goals of the people involved. Once this point is understood and accepted—and only when it is understood and accepted—an effective marketing program becomes possible.

To assist you in identifying what the real goals of your business are, I have provided The Business and Personal Goal Inventory worksheet.

Tool 3-B: The Business and Personal Goal Inventories

Figures 3.2 and 3.3 display the Business and Personal Goal Inventories. Starting with the Business Goal Inventory, try to identify each and every goal that your company has. Just list them in the left-hand column. If you need more space, use a second sheet. (If one of the goals I have specified does not apply, just cross it out.)

After you are finished listing the goals, briefly describe the specific criteria for the goal, if you know what it is. For example, if growth in sales volume is the goal, what level of growth are you shooting for? If it is, say 25 percent growth for calendar year 2009, write that under "Criteria."

Figure 3.2
Tool 3-B: Business Goal Inventory

		Importance to			
Goal	Criteria	Company	Management	Self	Comments

Figure 3.3
Tool 3-B: Personal Goal Inventory

Goal	Criteria		Importance to		Comments
		Community	Family	Self	

Figure 3.4
Sample Business Goal Inventory for Ted's Fish Market

Goal	Criteria	Importance to Company	Importance to Management	Importance to Self	Comments
Growth	Double revenue in two years	100%	30%	90%	Requires Loan
Expansion	Open 2 new locations in the next five years	90%	80%	80%	Opens new markets Upward path for new employees Need to start training managers
Tapping into the Tourist Market	Not sure	50%	?	?	Need to learn more Join Tourism Association
Improving Customer Service	Zero Customer Complaints	100%	100%	100%	Need to build reputation Customer Service Training Program
Expanding current Facility	Add anohter 2000 square feet	30%	40%	20%	Not sure what to do with the space Display Storage

Figure 3.5
Sample Personal Goal Inventory for Mike Jameson

Goal	Criteria	Importance to Company	Importance to Management	Importance to Self	Comments
Provide Security for family	My ownership stake worth $5 million by 50 years old	0%	100%	60%	
Maintain Family Life	Ask Wife Ask Children	0%	100%	100%	They Come First
Learn to Sail	Take Sailing Course in Annapolis, MD next summer	0%	50%	80%	Need a Hobby
Join Board of Not-For-Profit	Membership by the end of this year	80%	20%	60%	Ask Family what is important to them

In the next column, rate the goal on a scale of 0 percent to 100 percent according to your evaluation of how important the goal is to the company. It is important, however, that some thought go into this, because the total percentages should add up to 100 percent when you are done. This will give you an appreciation for the relative importance of the various goals that you have set or that have been set for you.

Next, rate the importance of each goal to your management. If you are management, rate the importance that you believe that you have communicated to your employees. In the final column, do the same thing, but this time rate each goal in terms of its importance to you personally.

The second worksheet is for your own personal goals as a member of the organization. Complete this worksheet in exactly the same manner. The only difference is that there is no column for identifying written goals.

Once you have completed the worksheets, take a hard look. First of all, what are the goals that you identified? Taken together, are they consistent? You may want to go through the five steps discussed earlier to do a more thorough evaluation of each goal.

Now look at the percentage ratings you have given to the importance of each goal to the company, management, and yourself. Are there any inconsistencies? How large are the inconsistencies? Any major inconsistencies in those ratings can indicate real or potential serious problems in achieving those goals as you, your management, and your organization are pulled in different directions.

Save these worksheets, we will be using them later.

Ted's Fish Market Example, in Figures 3.2 and 3.3, are examples of the ways Mike Jameson of Ted's Fish Market might have used these tools.

The Next Steps

The goals that you have identified will serve as guideposts for the development of your marketing strategies and tactics. At each step, you will be asking, "Does this marketing activity support my goals?" Remember that you need not set your goals in concrete. They should remain flexible as you figure out what you can and cannot accomplish with your marketing efforts.

The next two chapters show you how to identify and evaluate the most important source of resources for your organization: your customers.

SUMMARY

- ☑ Get clear about your goals
- ☑ Use the five-step goal-framing process
- ☑ Do a cost–benefit analysis on your goals

4

Your Market and What It Needs

The second step in our marketing analysis is identifying those in our environment who can help us reach our goals. We cannot achieve either our business or our personal goals without the help of others, for example, customers, suppliers, employees, financial institutions, government services, professional services, and so on.

We all understand on a personal level that we cannot achieve very much without the help of others: family, friends, teachers, significant others, and so on. And we know we have to choose these relationships carefully. The high divorce rate in this country demonstrates the cost of not being careful in our selections.

In addition, we cannot be all things to all people. We do not have the resources. Even if we had the resources, we do not have the time. We must choose, and choose wisely.

I cannot stress how important this analysis is. As entrepreneurs, we all have a tendency to focus on the critical/urgent tasks before us (as per Covey), and there are plenty of them! At the same time, our long-term success depends on finding our niche in the marketplace. We are most likely to find this place when we take the time, on an ongoing basis, to develop and refine our understanding of the business world in which we operate.

This chapter starts by identifying each of the key relationships a business must maintain to survive and succeed. Once these key relationships are identified, a series of processes are described to assist the reader to establish criteria for the selection of customers and business partners, and for the ongoing evaluation of existing and potential business relationships.

As we go through this analysis, it will be important to separate truth from desire. This means that for each external factor we consider, we must think in terms of both:

- The way we would like things to be, and
- The way things actually are.

YOUR EXTERNAL ENVIRONMENT

Your external environment consists of everything about your business world that you cannot operationally control. There are two major components:

1. *The marketplace:* This is the arena in which your product and services are sold. There are three components:

    - Customers: These are the people who already have purchased your product or service. Taking care of customers is crucial.
    - Potential customers: This is the focus of the rest of this chapter.
    - Competitors: This will be discussed in Chapter 7.

2. *Your operating environment:* This consists of all of the other organizations and people you need to make your organization work. For example:

    - Investors
    - Financial Institutions
    - Suppliers
    - Resellers
    - Government

The operating environment is discussed in the following chapter. For now, we are going to concentrate on the marketplace.

POTENTIAL CUSTOMERS

Now that you have your amazing product or service, your thoughts turn to finding the customers who will pay for it.

Your potential customer is anyone who might need something that you are willing and able to sell. That customer is the most important part of your business environment. Why? To paraphrase Willie Sutton, the famous bank robber: "That's where the money is!" And, unlike getting money from banks or investors, you don't have to give it back.

A "Good" Customer?

In particular, we are looking for someone (or some organization) that:

- Needs what you can provide.
- Derives value in excess of what your product or service would cost them.
- Has the resources to purchase.
- Is accessible to your marketing efforts.
- Can be adequately supported postsale.

All too often, identifying a good customer is given too little attention. It is easy to get enthusiastic about your own products and services and assume that other people would share that enthusiasm if only they knew about the product or service. The truth is that:

- People will only do business with you if they perceive it to be in their own interest to do so.
- The way people perceive their interests can be very complex and, potentially, contradictory. (Just like you.)
- People are very reluctant to change the way they do things, even in the face of information offering "a better way."

Your Best Customers

As I discussed in Chapter 2, it is easy to identify the largest demographic group you can that might be interested in what you have and decide that they are your target market. But this is a very expensive, inefficient, and usually ineffective way of approaching things.

What I said in Chapter 2 bears repeating here. The key to success is focusing on a customer group where you can be the best in some key area. As a new business, your best customers will be those that are unserved or underserved by your competition and among whom you can establish a clear advantage over those competitors.

This usually means that you find and focus upon a pond in which you can be the big fish. As your business, reputation, skills, and financial resources grow, you can always expand into other ponds. For right now, however, play the game you can win.

A SIX-STEP PROCESS FOR SELECTING TARGET MARKETS

As stated above, the selection of one or more key target markets for your marketing efforts is critical if you are going to use your marketing dollars efficiently. The six steps I propose are:

1. What potential market is there for your products and services?
2. How big is this market?
3. Why would potential customers in this market want your product or service?
4. What competitors would you face in this market?
5. How saturated is this market? (i.e., what percentage of the potential customers in this market already has or uses a competitive product or service?)
6. In what ways could you be special to the potential customers in this market?

Once you have identified a potential market for your company, you need to estimate how much potential you actually have to make profitable sales in that market.

Size is obviously important. But, as the story at the beginning of this chapter illustrated, there might be little potential even in a market that is considered large. If most people already have, and are satisfied with, a competitive product, there may be little potential for you, even in what seems to be a huge marketplace. Your only options are to tap into an unrecognized need (as we did in the story) or to offer an advantage that is so compelling that people will abandon your competitors and rush to buy from you. That is, of course, unless your competitors can simply match your offer to keep their customer base.

Your other option will be to find a smaller, but underserved market where you can become one of the dominant players, if not the dominant player. For the entrepreneur, this is usually the best chance for success.

IDENTIFYING POTENTIAL MARKETS

Your first task here is to identify as many potential markets for your products and services as you can. I have provided a worksheet for that purpose.

Tool 4-A: The Market Identification Worksheet

The Market Identification Worksheet (Figure 4.1) provides you a structured way to think expansively about your potential customer base(s).

The question is: Who might need something that you are willing and able to sell?

Have some fun with this. Get crazy! Try to identify every possibility you can, no matter how far-fetched.

For example, suppose you are in the business of making golf clubs. What potential markets do you have? Well, "golfers" comes immediately to mind. But there is a lot of competition out there selling golf clubs to ordinary golfers. So we ask "Are there any specific types of golfers that we could focus on?" Here is a partial list I came up with:

- Clubs for exceptionally short or tall golfers
- Clubs for golfers with physical disabilities
- Clubs for children
- Training clubs for strength building and/or rehabilitation
- Clubs to correct for chronic hooks or slices
- Extra lightweight clubs for the elderly
- Disposable clubs for people with tempers
- Clubs with heads and/or shafts in "designer" colors for people who want to be unique or stylish

Figure 4.1
Market Identification Worksheet

Who could use this?	Why?
1.	
2.	
3.	
4.	
5.	
6.	
7.	
8.	
9.	
10.	
11.	
12.	

- Custom clubs for organizations that want their logos or colors
- Clubs in exotic woods for people who want to be different
- Clubs that float (also for people with tempers or who are klutzes).

But wait! If you can make golf clubs, you must have some core skills in woodworking and metalworking. In particular, you are probably very good at making 3″ to 5″ long, lumpy objects out of various metals, maybe even titanium. You could ask yourself who might need these kinds of things. Could you make:

- Parts for automobiles, appliances, or other products?
- Parts for aircraft (titanium)?
- Paperweights?
- Ammunition?
- Tools?

At this point you should have an interesting list of potential markets for your products. Hopefully, you have identified at least ten. If it's fewer than ten, go back and think again. Ask your employees, ask your friends, ask your suppliers. Leave no stone unturned. Also, remember that this is intended to be an ongoing process. You can (and should) go back and add new potential markets whenever they occur to you.

Ted's Fish Market Example: Figure 4.2 shows the Market Identification Worksheet as it might have been filled out by Mike Jameson, owner of Ted's Fish Market.

Figure 4.2
Market Identification Worksheet for Ted's Fish Market—Fresh Caught New England Fish

Who could use this?	Why?
1. Restaurants	Customer—Quality
2. Caterers	Customers—Quality
3. Families	Meals
4. Couples	Special occasions, parties
5. Singles	Parties, special occasions
6. Tourists	Gifts, take home
7. Gourmets	Want the best quality
8. Food Services	Hospitals, schools, etc. Long term contract, low price

ASSESSING MARKET OPPORTUNITIES: POWERFUL, INEXPENSIVE MARKET RESEARCH TECHNIQUES

Market research has an undeservedly bad reputation. Most people consider it to be complex, difficult, and expensive. The good news, however, is that:

- Market research, like so much else in business adheres to the 80/20 rule. You can usually get about 80 percent of the information you need with about 20 percent of the total effort required.
- There is a vast array of free information resources available to you.

In this section, I suggest some inexpensive ways you can quickly obtain a great deal of information.

Internal Sources

Companies usually know a great deal more about their market than they think they know. Here are some of the internal sources that I usually go to when I am working with companies.

1. *Sales records*: If you have been in business for a while, you already have a great source of information in the sales records you have. If they have been entered into some kind of database (e.g., QuickBooks) you can find out a lot about your customers including:
   - What they buy
   - At what price
   - When they buy
   - Geographic locations
   - Customer demographics
   - And so on.

In large corporations, this is called "data mining," and software (usually expensive software) exists to help with this effort. However, I have found that simply laying the information out in a spreadsheet can often lead to very interesting insights.

I once worked with a car dealership where its predominant customer base had changed, geographically and demographically, over a period of years. However, management had not paid attention to that change and was still advertising to the former customer types in the former locations and wondering why sales were declining. Two hours in their filing cabinet was all it took to discover the truth.

2. *Salespeople:* Your salespeople are your frontline troops. They are the ones talking with potential customers every day, learning about their needs and product preferences. Salespeople can be an exceedingly valuable source of information about unmet market needs, desirable product/service upgrades, and competitive action.

   I recommend that you not only debrief your salespeople from time to time, but that you also make them a core part of your ongoing information gathering effort.

3. *Customer service people:* Customer service people have a tough job. People rarely call in to tell them how great your product is. These people get to hear about all the negative things. At the same time, customers with problems will talk about those problems. Wouldn't it be good to know what they are talking about so that you can do something about those problems?

   Again, make your customer service people part of your data gathering effort. Talk to them. Ask them questions. Listen to what they have to say. Ask them to help gather other information you might need. After all, they have a customer on the phone, why not ask one or two more questions?

4. *Customers:* If you have been doing your job and keeping your customers happy, these are your best friends. I have constantly been amazed and delighted by the extent to which happy customers will help. In particular, you can often get them to share information with you about:

   - Your own strengths and weaknesses
   - Competitive products, pricing, marketing, and sales activities
   - Your (and your competitors') reputation in the marketplace
   - Potential new directions to take your products and your marketing activities
   - Potential new markets for your products and services.

Secondary Data

Market researchers talk about two kinds of data:

- Primary data: Data that you gather yourself
- Secondary data: Data that someone else has already gathered and that you can potentially obtain

Primary data is usually more complicated and costly to obtain, so I will leave that discussion for later and concentrate on the many ways you can obtain secondary data, often for free.

Publications

America is a country of writers. There seems to be almost no topic upon which some subset of our population will not base a newspaper, magazine, newsletter, Web site, or blog.

According to the Standard Rate and Data Service (SRDS), as of 2008, there are approximately 6,100 newspapers and 12,000 magazines published in the United States. And there are many more than that published throughout the world. In addition, there are literally thousands of academic journals. Obviously, a huge amount of information is contained in these pages.

Fortunately, you do not have to read through it all to get what information might pertain to your markets and your industry. Most of this information is available through online databases. The bad news is that these databases require a paid subscription before they allow access. The good news is that many public colleges and many public libraries have these subscriptions and will allow you to use them for free. You may even be able to obtain access at home or at work through your local public library.

For example, at Kutztown University, where I have taught several marketing courses, we have several of these databases, including Academic Search Complete (by EBSCO Host). This database contains more than 5,300 full-text periodicals, including 4,400 peer-reviewed academic journals. In addition to full text, this database offers indexing and abstracts for more than 9,300 journals and a total of 10,900 publications including monographs, reports, conference proceedings, and so on. The database features PDF content going back as far as 1865, with the majority of full text titles in native (searchable) PDF format. This database also includes popular titles such as *Time*, *Newsweek*, and *Business Week*.

A discussion of other sources of published information is included in Chapter 7.

Government Sources

The range of data collected and maintained by the government is mind-boggling. Among my favorites are:

- Department of Commerce (www.doc.gov)
    - Census Bureau (http://www.census.gov)
    - Bureau of Economic Analysis (http://www.bea.gov)
    - U.S. Patent and Trademark Office (http://www.uspto.gov)
- Securities and Exchange Commission (www.sec.gov)
- Small Business Administration (www.sba.gov)

- Office of Small Business Development Centers (http://www.sba.gov/aboutsba/sbaprograms/sbdc/index.html)
- Kutztown University Small Business Development Center (http://www.kutztownsbdc.org)

It would take another whole book to adequately describe all of the valuable information that you can gain from these sites. I strongly recommend that you check out each of the above Web sites and just spend some time exploring.

Nongovernment Sources

1. *Trade associations*: There are over 135,000 nonprofit associations worldwide, coving an extremely wide array of subjects. Of these, some 22,300 are U.S. national associations. Many of these publish magazine, newsletters, papers on special interests, and/or membership directories.

   You can find most of these by looking them up in the *Encyclopedia of Associations*. This set of books is usually available in hard copy at college libraries and many public libraries. It can also be accessed online through Lexis-Nexis.
2. *Colleges and universities*: In addition to their library resources, colleges and universities can also be a major source of business information and education. Check your local area colleges for:

   - Workshops and seminars
   - Entrepreneurship institutes
   - Small Business Development Center consulting programs
   - Faculty experts in industry areas
   - Research programs in areas relevant to your business or industry.

Experts

Experts are individuals who are likely to have knowledge of and insights into potential target markets for your products and services. There are two types of experts: professional and nonprofessional.

Professional experts (also called "consultants") usually charge a fee for sharing their knowledge and insights. Fees might range from nothing (for an initial meeting) up to hundreds of dollars per hour or thousands per day. However, when considering using a paid expert, think in terms of the value of the information they could provide and the amount of money you could save by not having to go out and collect the information yourself, rather than the hourly fee. Good consultants have spent huge amounts of time developing their knowledge and skills; you can reap those benefits in just a short amount of time.

Nonprofessional experts are other people who are in a position to provide you some information or insight about your market. These include:

- Retired people
- Executives in customer firms

- Salespeople for other types of products being sold into your market
- Bankers and other financial advisors
- Community leaders
- Trade association staff
- Chamber of Commerce staff
- Your suppliers
- Friends, colleagues, and others with whom you can share ideas
- Government employees
    - Federal government agencies
    - State and local government economic development staff

The best way to gather information is, of course, to ask questions and then listen to the answers. If you are looking to gather information, it is vital that you suppress your natural enthusiasm for discussing your own company and products. Make these discussions about your source and his/her perspectives. If you and they want to have a conversation about you and your business, try to schedule it for another time. In that way your initial conversation will remain focused on getting the outside perspectives you need.

Also, talk to as many people as you reasonably can. Everyone has their own perspective and, even if they are considered to be experts, there are biases, gaps of knowledge, and "ego" in anyone you talk with.

As you read more and listen more, you will begin to find a pattern emerging in all that information. That is the "gold" you are seeking.

Market Research Firms

If looking at the available information out there and talking to people who can provide you insight and perspective are not sufficient for your purposes, you can obtain the assistance of a professional market research firm. Some of the tools of the research firm include:

- *Focus groups*: A focus group typically consists of five to ten individuals who are gathered in a room to discuss a particular issue or product. Individuals who are knowledgeable about the product and/or are potential purchasers of the product are recruited to participate, and the discussion is moderated by a skilled facilitator who tries to ensure that everyone's opinions are elicited. Usually, you, as the client, will sit behind a one-way mirror and observe the discussion. I have found focus groups to be a simple, powerful, and relatively inexpensive method for gathering information.
- *Intercept surveys*: Have you ever been shopping and had someone with a clipboard comes up to you and ask you if "you would mind answering just a couple of quick questions?" This research technique is called an "intercept study." The idea is that a mall, trade show, sporting event, or other type of gathering gets like-minded people in one place. They can then be easily surveyed.

- *Telephone surveys*: The use of telephone surveys has been declining in recent years for two reasons: past abuses of people using them as a pretext for sales pitches, and the advent of "do not call" lists. Although relatively inexpensive and fast, I generally no longer recommend this approach unless you have a qualified list of people with a reasonable expectation of interest in the subject.
- *Face-to-face interviews*: This is the most expensive yet potentially most effective method for gathering information about market needs. It involves interviewers scheduling meetings, traveling to the person's location, and taking the time to do a one-on-one discussion. Although this method is powerful and provides the best opportunity for statistically reliable data, it can cost up to several hundred dollars per respondent.

MARKET SEGMENTATION AND TARGETING

The third and last part of this chapter discusses the processes known as market segmentation and targeting. The basic premises here are:

- You can't be everything to everybody.
- You don't have enough resources to try.
- So, figure out where you get the biggest bang for your buck.

Segmentation: Sorting Your Potential Market into Meaningful Groups

The first step in this process is to consider the ways in which your potential market could be further broken down into meaningful groups. Marketers call this the process of "segmentation."

What makes a group "meaningful?" A subgroup of your potential market is meaningful to the extent that it might require:

- Its own unique or tailored marketing approach.
- An expansion of your basic marketing approach in order to reach that group more effectively.

I understand that these ideas may seem vague or complex at first, but they are important to understand, and I attempt to clarify them in this and later chapters.

Ted's Fish Market Example: When Mike Jameson at Ted's went through this process, he realized that there were actually five distinctly different types of customer that he had. He gave these customer types the following names:

- *Commercial customers*: Restaurants and caterers who regularly buy seafood in bulk on order. These customers account for about 40 percent of Ted's business.
- *Locals*: People who live or work nearby and use Ted's as a primary source of seafood. This type of customer accounts for about 20 percent of business.

- *Partiers*: People who make a special trip to Ted's to pick up larger amounts of seafood for parties and cookouts. These customers usually account for 10 percent to 15 percent of Ted's business, but that can go way up for holidays and special events such as the Super Bowl.
- *Gourmets*: People who come to Ted's because the fish is much fresher than that in grocery stores. These customers account for about 20 percent of sales.
- *Tourists*: People from out of town who think it's cool to buy fish from an old, authentic New England fish market. These customers represent 5 percent to 10 percent of sales, depending on the time of year.

Segmenting by Customer Differences

The most effective way to segment your market is to look for fundamental differences among your current and potential customers. Some of these differences could be in wants and needs, ability to service, buying behavior, or accessibility to influence.

- Wants and needs: Different parts of the marketplace may want different things from your product or service. At the beginning of this book, I said that customers do not buy a product or service, they buy an "anticipated experience." Consider the differences that might exist in the needs that are satisfied by the product or the ways in which the product is used. In the story at the beginning of Chapter 8, I divided the market for home heating oil into the three basic reasons why someone would enter into a new contract: buying a house, attempting to save money, dissatisfaction with current supplier.
- Ability to service: Just because someone may want what you have doesn't mean you are going to be able to supply that need, even if the potential customer expressed a desire to buy from you. There are two basic reasons you might not be able to provide for a customer: capability and geography. In some cases, you may not be big enough nor have the range of product service offerings that a potential customer might need. This issue is discussed in Chapter 6. On the other hand, potential customers might be too far away, especially if you are providing personal or professional services.
- Buying behavior: Different customers buy in different ways. For example, some people want to take their time and shop around, while others are more time sensitive than price sensitive. Some customers are perfectly happy to buy all kinds of products (including automobiles and furniture) over the Internet while others (like me) want to see the product with their own eyes before making a major investment.
- Accessibility to influence: Just as there are people who buy for different reasons, there are people who are influenced for different reasons and by different methods. Examples of different influence methods include:
  - Advertising
  - Referrals from friends

- Personal experience and product trials
- Positive third-party recommendations
- Positive evaluations from consumer or trade publications (e.g., *Consumer Reports*)

Other Segmentation Techniques

Although segmenting by actual differences sounds sensible, it may sometimes be impractical. Relevant factors, such as price sensitivity, are often difficult to measure for specific people. What marketers usually end up doing is using more easily measured factors that can be expected to correlate closely with the underlying factors of importance.

For example, we might reasonably expect people who live in areas with higher-priced homes to be more affluent, and therefore less price sensitive, than people who live in areas with lower-priced homes. This method for segmentation works only in the aggregate. Just because someone lives in an expensive house does not mean either that they have a lot of money (they could have inherited it or have bought it years ago before the neighborhood became so expensive) or that they are not price sensitive (they could be "house poor" or just very careful with their money, which is how they can afford that nice house).

Some of the more generic methods marketers use to segment include:

- Geographic segmentation: The easiest way to segment a market is by geographic area. This is best used when:
  - Your firm has limited ability to deliver and support products and services.
  - You rely on regionally based advertising media like newspapers, TV, and radio.
  - Product/service demand or usage patterns vary by locality.
- Demographic segmentation: Demographic segmentation is one of the most popular methods of market segmentation. It consists of dividing up the market by basic population characteristics such as:
  - Age
  - Gender
  - Race/ethnicity
  - Marital status
  - Family size
  - Income
  - Education
- The idea is that certain product/service needs, buying patterns, values, and wealth vary by some of these characteristics.
- Psychographic segmentation: Psychographic segmentation gets closer to actual need/usage patterns by dividing up the marketplace in terms of psychological or behavioral characteristics.

- Very often these groups are defined and organized in the context of the actual product or service offered. The groups are then given descriptive names to reflect their main character.
- For example, BMW segments its market into the following groups:
  - Upper liberals: open-minded, socially aware professionals
  - Postmoderns: High-earning individualists
  - Upper conservatives: Wealthy traditionalists
  - Modern mainstream: Families who can only afford entry level luxury cars.

Assessing Segment Attractiveness

The next step toward defining your target market(s) is to assess the "attractiveness" of each of the segments you identified.

The criteria used to identify segment attractiveness were identified at the beginning of this chapter.

1. How big is each market?
2. Why would potential customers in each of these markets want your product or service?
3. What competitors would you face in each market?
4. How saturated is each market? (i.e., what percentage of each market already has a similar product or is using a similar service?)
5. In what ways could you be special to the potential customers in each of these markets?

I wish I could give you some kind of mathematical algorithm you could use to assess segment attractiveness, but I can't. What you have to do is:

1. Think
2. Gather information
3. Think
4. Ask people
5. Think
6. Notice what information you are missing
7. Think some more
8. Make a decision and act.

And at the same time, don't try to overanalyze this process. If you are thorough, the patterns will emerge.

Tool 4-B: The Segmentation Process Worksheet

The Segmentation Process Worksheet is shown in Figure 4.3. This worksheet will help guide you through the process of segmentation and targeting.

Figure 4.3
The Segmentation Process Worksheet

	Segment	Segment Attractiveness			
		Suitability	Growth	Accessibility	Competition
1					
2					
3					
4					
5					
6					

Figure 4.4
Segmentation Process Worksheet for Ted's Fish Market

	Segment	Segment Attractiveness			
		Suitability	Growth	Accessibility	Competition
1	Commercial Customers	Medium	Medium	Medium- Takes a Sales Call	SYSCO, ARAMARK
2	Locals	High - Very Convenient	Low	High	Other Fish Markets Grocery Stores
3	Partiers	High - Will pay for Quality	Medium	High	Fish Markets Grocery Stores
4	Gourmets	High - Will pay for Quality	High	Medium- Takes a Srong Appeal	Fish Markets Gourmet Stores
5	Tourists	High- Will pay Top Dollar	High	Medium - Not right in town	Gift Shops
6	Food Services	Low - Lowprofit Potential	Medium	Low - Long term Bid Contracts	Large Providers of Foreign Fish

The steps will help you to:

- Define segmentation criteria
- Identify segments
- Assess segment attractiveness
  - Product/service suitability
  - Growth
  - Accessibility
  - Competition
- Select segments to target

Ted's Fish Market Example: Figure 4.4 shows how the Segmentation Process Worksheet could have been filled out for Ted's Fish Market.

Currently, locals are their primary target market, with some sales going to commercial customers. However, the chart suggests that gourmets and tourists could be excellent markets for expansion. Food services, on the other hand, would probably not be worth the effort.

SUMMARY

☑ Look for "good" customers.
☑ Use the six-step process for identifying target markets.
☑ Tap your internal sources of information first.
☑ Take advantage of the many free external sources of information.
☑ There are a lot of experts who might be willing to help you for free.
☑ Use research firms only if you really need to.
☑ Segment your market into meaningful groups.
☑ Target the best segments for your marketing program.
☑ Tailor your program to those segments.

5

Your Operational Environment

Although your market is probably the most important part of your external environment (and therefore deserving of its own chapter), there is much more to be considered. This chapter helps you take a step back and look at the wider landscape of the business environment in which you operate.

There are two sections to this chapter:

1. A general discussion of the other, nonmarket aspects of your business environment, and
2. The presentation of a powerful analytical tool to help you make an overall assessment of your external world.

THE EXTERNAL ENVIRONMENT

The success of any entrepreneurial venture relies on much more than identifying an underserved market need and developing a quality product or service in response. In today's increasingly complex business climate, entrepreneurs must establish and maintain relationships with a wide array of other organizations including investors, suppliers, resellers, banks, and government.

Too many entrepreneurs take these ancillary relationships lightly. That can be a big mistake. It is vitally important that, whenever possible, you carefully select every component of your external environment and that you create and maintain effective relationships with each of these individuals and organizations.

There is not enough space in this book to go into detail about each component of your personal business world, so I am going to simply list and briefly describe each. Take the time to reflect on each key individual or organization in your world and whether your relationship with them is truly serving your goals. I have also provided a worksheet to help you.

Business Associates

We are not in this alone. To operate, you need to have strong relationships with a number of organizations and groups, each of which provides critical operational resources to you. The following list of organizations and individuals is not intended to be required or exhaustive, but rather an extensive array of possibilities.

- Business Partners
  - Distribution Channel (resellers, agents, shippers)
  - Supply chain (raw materials, components and subassembly manufacturers, contract manufacturers, technical subcontractors, operational and office support subcontractors)
- Stockholders
  - Individuals (partners, friends, & family)
  - Angel investors
  - Venture capitalists
  - Investment houses
- Banks
  - Lenders
  - Credit card processors
  - Factoring entities (short term lending on receivables)
- Employees
  - Rank & file
  - Professionals (internal professionals, accountants, lawyers)
  - Managers
  - Labor unions

Other Environmental Entities

This list encompasses the other external entities that can have a significant impact on your operational and financial success.

- Competitors (see Chapter 7)
- Government
  - Regulatory agencies (IRS, OSHA, SBA, any specifically relevant to your industry such as Agriculture, Energy, Defense)
  - National policy (interest rates, international trade, consumer confidence)
  - State & local government (licensing, taxation, zoning, local operational regulations)
- Trade associations
  - Your industry
  - Your customers' industries (if customers are businesses)
- Special interest groups

- Especially if your business or operations are in any way controversial (pharmaceuticals, certain medical specialties, energy)

Tool 5-A: The Business Environment Inventory Worksheet

I provided a worksheet (Figure 5.1) to help you identify the relevant aspects of your business environment. I recommend that you use this worksheet to take a thorough inventory of all of the various organizations and individuals outside of your company that have, or could have, an impact, positive or negative, on your success.

As you go through this worksheet, rate each component of your business environment on a scale of 1 to 10 (where 10 is *high*) in terms of (1) the relevance of that component of your environment to your business success and (2) your assessment of the quality of that component. If that component is irrelevant to you, just put in an "*N*."

In the next section, I present an analytical tool you can use to evaluate how friendly or hostile your overall environment is.

Ted's Fish Market Example: Figure 5.2 displays Mike Jameson's first attempt to complete the Business Environment Inventory Worksheet. Note that he currently operates in a rather simple business environment. Should he choose to expand by opening new locations or offering proprietary products of his own (e.g., spices), he would soon find the need for attorneys (real estate and intellectual property), accountants (to establish a more sophisticated bookkeeping system), marketing professionals, and a new banker.

ASSESSING YOUR EXTERNAL ENVIRONMENT

It would be nice to have a way to make an overall assessment of the extent to which your chosen environment is either friendly or hostile to you and your goals. Fortunately, such a tool exists. It is called the "External Factor Evaluation" or EFE.

Opportunities and Threats

In Chapter 2, I discussed the SWOT Analysis. The External Factor Evaluation (EFE) is based on SWOT.

In the EFE, we look only at the external side of the process: your opportunities and threats. To review:

- An opportunity is an aspect of the external environment that is, or could be, favorable to your company
- A Threat is an aspect of the external environment that is, or could be, a problem for your company

A Note about Analytical Tools

Regarding analytical models, keep in mind that the primary purpose of the analytical models is to get the right questions asked. It is not about

Figure 5.1
Business Environment Inventory Worksheet

Business Associates	Relevance	Rating	Notes
Professional Support			
Accountants			
Lawyers			
Business Consultants			
Supply Chain			
Raw Materials			
Components & Subassemblies			
Contract Manufacturers			
Technical Consultants			
Operational and Office Support Subcontractors			
Other			
Distribution Channel			
Resellers			
Independent Sales Agents			
Shippers			
Financial			
Investors			
Individuals			
Angel Investors			
Venture Capitalists			
Investment Houses			
Other			

Figure 5.1 (*Continued*)

	Relevance	Rating	Notes
Banks			
Business Accounts			
Lenders			
Credit Card Procesors			
Factoring			
Government			
Regulatory Agencies			
OSHA			
Other			
State & Local			
Licensing			
Taxation			
Zoning			
Local Operational Regulations			
Other			
Trade Associations			
Your Industry			
Customer's Industry			
Special Interest Groups			

getting the right answers. If you ask the right questions, the answers regarding what is going on in your business world and what you should do about it become clear.

Next, the value of the results is entirely dependent on the information entered. Data analysts use the acronym "GIGO." It stands for garbage in = garbage out. That is why it is so important that you are careful about what you include in your analyses.

Next, don't confuse assumptions and judgments with facts. There are really two issues here. First, you will never have all of the facts you need to make an airtight decision. You will always have to depend on the judgments and assumptions of yourself and others. At the same time, you need

Figure 5.2
Business Environment Inventory for Ted's Fish Market

Business Associates	Relevance	Rating	Notes
Professional Support	2	6	
Accountants	2	5	
Lawyers	2	7	
Business Consultants	N		
Supply Chain			
Raw Materials	10	9	Fish From Suppliers
Components & Subassemblies	N		
Contract Manufacturers	N		
Technical Consultants	N		
Operational and Office Support Subcontractors	N		
Other	N		
Distribution Channel			
Resellers	N		
Independent Sales Agents	N		
Shippers	N		
Financial			
Investors			
Individuals	9	8	Fathter still owns 49%
Angel Investors	N		
Venture Capitalists	N		
Investment Houses	N		
Other	N		
Banks			
Business Accounts	4	8	Bank is fine
Lenders	9	4	Other thanoperating line, need loan to grow, bank is reticent
Credit Card Processors	3	8	
Factoring	N		

Figure 5.2 (*Continued*)

Government	Relevance	Rating	Notes
Regulatory Agencies	N		
OSHA	N		
Other	N		
State & Local	4	6	
Licensing	4	6	
Taxation	4	6	
Zoning	9	8	Town seems amenable to my expansion
Local Operational Regulations	N		
Other			
Trade Associations	N		
Your Industry	?		Have not investigated joining, Look at tourism council
Customer's Industry	N		
Special Interest Groups	N		

to recognize that someone's judgment, no matter how well informed, is still a judgment, not a fact. These assumptions and judgments provide the most powerful insights and most potential for error.

Next, try the models different ways. As you go through the various analyses I present in this book, try them out with different assumptions, different factors, and different evaluations. See what, if any, differences you get in your results.

Finally, you are never done with your analysis. The use of these analytical tools should be an ongoing process. As you continue to learn about yourself, your markets, your competitors, and the rest of your operational environment, keep updating your analyses. Notice what changes. Notice how much you have learned. Refocus your energies into learning even more.

Tool 5-B: External Factor Evaluation

In a nutshell, the EFE puts numbers to the opportunities and threats you have identified. Figure 5.3 is a worksheet you can use.

The analysis itself is done in the following steps:

- Step 1: Select the most important external factors you need to consider. The first step of this analysis is to identify the most important issues in

Figure 5.3
External Factor Evaluation

For each Identified Factor:
How would you categorize it?
Major Opportunity = 4 | Minor Threat = 2
Minor Opportunity = 3 | Major Threat = 1
How important is that factor? | Rate from 1-10, 10 being most important

External Factors	Factor Value (FV) (1-4)	Factor Weight (FW) (1-10)	Normalized Factor Weight (NW) =FW/TW	Weighted Factor =FV*NW
1				
2				
3				
4				
5				
6				
Sums				

your external environment: the issues that get entered into this analysis. The list of opportunities and threats you identified for your SWOT Analysis in Chapter 2 is a good starting point. Refine this list with what you have learned about your marketplace (Chapter 4) and the rest of your external environment at the beginning of this chapter. Include competitive factors also, although you will be refining these in the following chapter.

Unlike the other lists we have compiled so far, this list of key external factors should be selective, not exhaustive. As a starting point, try to select the six to eight most important factors. You can always add more at a later time. Try to identify those aspects of your environment that really make a difference to you. An important part of this exercise is going through the thinking that leads to creating this list.

- Step 2: Assign a weight for each factor. The factors you have chosen, even though they are the most critical for you, probably vary in their overall level of importance. So take a minute and assign each of those factors a rating of 1 to 10 with 1 being the lowest level of importance and 10 being the highest. Rate each independently. Don't try to prioritize them.

The next step is the most difficult arithmetic procedure in this entire book. You need to compute the percentage of the total weight that the weight of each factor represents. It is actually quite straightforward. Suppose you selected the following factors for your analysis:

1. Underserved market for people older than age 55
2. Easing of government regulations
3. Reseller network

4. Largest competitor having financial problems
5. Competitive start-up firm has patented new technology

You then assign each of these factors a weight:

Underserved market for people older than age 55	9
Easing of government regulations	5
Reseller network	4
Largest competitor having financial problems	7
Competitive start-up firm has patented new technology	10
Total	35

The total of the weights you have assigned is 35 (9 + 5 + 4 + 7 + 10). All you have to do is compute the percentage each weight is of the total weights. This process is called "normalization" by statisticians. For example, the normalized weight for factor 1 is 25.7 percent (9 divided by 35).

The final chart would look like this:

Underserved market for people older than age 55	9	25.7%
Easing of government regulations	5	14.3%
Reseller network	4	11.4%
Largest competitor having financial problems	7	20.0%
Competitive start-up firm has patented new technology	10	28.6%
Total	35	100.0%

- Step 3: Assign a value for each factor. The next step is to assign a value to each of the factors, indicating the extent to which each represents an opportunity or a threat to you. You can use almost any scale you feel comfortable with. (For example, you can use a scale of 0 to 100 with 0 indicating a dire threat and 100 representing an amazing opportunity.) However, for learning purposes, I initially recommend the following simple scale:

  - 4 = Major opportunity
  - 3 = Minor opportunity
  - 2 = Minor threat
  - 1 = Major threat

- Step 4: Multiply and sum. In the final step of this analysis, simply multiply the factor value (1 to 4) that you just assigned by the percentage weight of the factor. Sum these up to get a snapshot of the friendliness of your business environment.

Figure 5.4
External Factor Evaluation for Ted's Fish Market

External Factors	Factor Value (FV) (1-4)	Factor Weight (FW) (1-10)	Normalized Factor Weight (NW) =FW/TW	Weighted Factor =FV*NW
1 Increasing tourism	4	7	19.4%	0.778
2 Increasing consumption of fish	4	9	25.0%	1.000
3 Boutiques store rising	3	3	8.3%	0.250
4 Area economically healthy	3	5	13.9%	0.417
5 Improving neighborhoods	3	4	11.1%	0.333
6 Dependency on foreign fisheries	1	3	8.3%	0.083
7 Globalwarming	2	3	8.3%	0.167
8 Govt regulation	2	2	5.6%	0.111
	Sums	36	100.0%	3.139

A final value close to 4 indicates a very positive business environment and a value close to 1 indicates a very hostile environment. Most scores end up between 2 and 3. Scores above 2.5 indicate a generally positive environment. Scores above 3 indicate a very positive business environment. Scores less than 2.5 indicate below average environments.

Ted's Fish Market Example: Figure 5.4 shows the completed chart for Ted's Fish Market including all calculations.

The final number, 3.139, indicates that Ted's business environment is quite positive. Also note that the issues used were drawn directly from the SWOT Analysis.

- Step 5: Validation. Now that you have arrived at a number, you get to ask the all-important question: "Does this number make sense?"

  Whether you have been in business for 30 years or 30 days, you probably have some sense as to the whether you are in a friendly or hostile environment. Did the number you came up with agree with your expectations? Does it agree with your experience?

If the answers are "no," there can be only two reasons:

1. You have not included the most relevant factors in your analysis. If this is the case, you have more to learn about your markets, competitors, or operational environment.
2. You don't know as much as you think you know. If this is the case, you have even more to learn about your markets, competitors, or operational environment.

If it makes you feel any better, in my consulting experience, I have found that almost all entrepreneurs have at least one important blind spot in their view of themselves and the world. The successful ones understand that and are constantly trying to learn as much as they can.

SUMMARY

- ☑ Your operating environment encompasses much more than just your market and your competitors
- ☑ Good relationships with all aspects of your environment are essential

6

Assessing Your Own Capabilities

So far, you have:

- Clarified your personal and professional goals,
- Examined your market, segmented, and chosen one or more target markets, and
- Reviewed the remainder of your business environment.

Now, it is time to take a hard look at yourself and your business. You know what your opportunities are. What can you deliver? In particular, what can you do better than anyone else?

When I was a professor at the University of Maryland, I received a referral to a store that sold landscaping materials: paving stones, gravel, lawn ornaments, and so on. I called the owner and, because he was about 45 minutes away, I made arrangements to visit him later in the week.

When working with retail establishments, I usually like to visit it first in the role of a customer so I can get the feel of the place before I meet the owner. In this case, I showed up twenty minutes early for the meeting, dressed in casual clothes.

A walk around the facility left me appalled. What had once obviously been a beautiful garden spot had seriously decayed. Lawn ornaments had fallen over. Paving stones had hand-painted price signs, and some of the signs had misspellings. The two koi ponds were empty of water and had trash in them. Weeds were everywhere. There was a small building that served as an office and a showroom for decorative kerosene heaters. The place reeked of fuel oil. The chairs in the office were tattered.

The owner, however, was delightful. A man in his late sixties, he had owned the facility for many years. I introduced myself and asked him to describe his problem. He told me that his sales were declining. The reasons he gave included a bad local economy, competitive pressure, and a change in traffic patterns that made his place hard to see until one was almost on top of it.

After listening patiently to his story for about fifteen minutes, I said simply: "That's not it." When he started to object, I asked him to follow me outside. I took him on a tour of his own shop, showing him the fallen ornaments, misspelled signs, and trash-filled koi ponds. He was astounded! Apparently the deterioration had taken place over such a long period that he literally had not seen it. He called over his assistant and we went around one more time. Then I left. There was nothing more I could do for him right then. Before he could or should do anything else to restore sales, he needed to realize, once again, what a great place he had, and to treat it as such.

That week, he hired a young man through a county program for unemployed youth. When I went to visit him again a month later, the place was transformed. It looked like something out of a magazine. There were new displays, new signs, koi ponds with koi swimming around in them. And sales were picking back up.

COMPETENCIES

Let's move back a step from your specific product or service and start with the idea of competence. In other words, what are you good at? Business analysts look at three levels of competence:

- Basic competence
- Core competence
- Distinctive competence.

A basic competency is anything that you and your company are good at doing. This includes essential tasks such as production and marketing and less important tasks such as emptying trash cans.

Core competencies are those skills necessary to your business. These can include product design, production, marketing, and customer support. These are the skills that you (and your competitors) must have to function effectively in your industry.

What makes a core competency different from a basic competency is that your core competencies cannot (or should not) be outsourced. You can easily hire someone to come in and clean your offices, do your bookkeeping, or ship your products to customers. It is much more difficult to outsource product design or marketing strategy (although it is certainly possible to get outside professional assistance).

Your distinctive competencies are what can make you unique in the marketplace. These are the things you do better than anyone else. (More about this later.)

Tool 6-A: Competency Inventories

Just to get an initial picture of what you think you can do, make a list of all of the things that you and your company can do. Make these separate lists for yourself and your organization. I have provided sample forms for your use: Figures 6.1 and 6.2. Although the forms have only 12 rows, you may use as many rows as you want.

Figure 6.1
Tool 6-A: Personal Competency Inventory

No.	Competency	Core?	Distv?
1			
2			
3			
4			
5			
6			
7			
8			
9			
10			
11			
12			

- *Step 1*: Put down everything you can think of. Treat this like a brainstorming session and don't edit yourself. The more items you include, the better. Identify whatever you or your company is good at whether or not you think that skill is relevant to your business success.

Think carefully. Take some time. Ask your employees. Ask your customers.

As I said earlier in this book, you (and your company) are much more competent than you are probably giving yourself credit for. So here's your chance to identify and to ''own'' all the great things you can do!

For inspiration, I like the following quote: ''If it's true, it ain't bragging.'' (Mark Twain)

Figure 6.2
Tool 6-A: Organizational Competency Inventory

No.	Competency	Core?	Distv?
1			
2			
3			
4			
5			
6			
7			
8			
9			
10			
11			
12			

- *Step 2*: Review the list. Identify those competencies that are essential to your effective functioning in your business world. Then, from that list, identify those things that you do extraordinarily well.
- *Step 3*: Review the list again. This time look for things that you or your company may be exceptionally good at but that do not seem relevant to your business. These are your untapped personal and organizational resources. Although it is not necessary (or even desirable) to use all your skills in business, it is certainly important to know they are there.

Ted's Fish Market Examples: Examples of how these Competency Inventories might be done for Ted's Fish Market are shown in Figures 6.3 and 6.4.

Figure 6.3
Personal Competency Inventory for Mike Jameson

No.	Competency	Core?	Distv?
1	Buy Quality Fish at good prices	X	
2	Manage a Small Business	X	
3	Work with customers	X	
4	Preparation of Fish - Spices and Specialty recipes Attended Culinary School		X
5	Knowledge of Wine		X
6	Entrepeneurial Spirit		X
7	Facility with Accounting Software	X	
8	Recruiting and Managing Good Employees	X	
9			

ORGANIZATIONAL RESOURCES

As you have discovered, there is a whole lot to developing a strategic marketing plan for your business beyond coming up with a great idea for a product or service. The next step in your analysis is to take a long, hard look at the resources that you can bring to bear to meet customer needs.

Tool 6-B: The Organizational Resource Inventory

Figure 6.5 is an Organizational Resource Inventory for you to go through. This inventory covers a wide range of issues that may (or may not) be relevant to your business strength. Categories include:

- Physical assets
- Production capability
- Customer support capability
- Personnel
- Intellectual capital
- Customer base

Figure 6.4
Organizational Competency Inventory for Ted's Fish Market

No.	Competency	Core?	Distv?
1	Customer Service	X	
2	Fresh Fish	X	
3	Store Layout	X	
4	Local Advertising	X	
5	Consistent Profitability	X	
6	Historic Facility	X	
7	Employee Job Security	X	
8			

- Product/service lines
- Brands
- Alliances

I have tried to identify as many issues as I can for you, but there are probably other issues relevant to your particular situation that I have missed. There are blank lines for you to fill in so you can add more issues as they occur to you.

Rate each item on the list as one of the following:

1. Best in industry
2. Excellent
3. Adequate
4. Needs improvement
5. Not in place
6. Irrelevant

For those issues you rate either 1 or 4, you should make a note as to why you rated it that way.

Tool 6-C: The Four-Point Test for Business Strengths

There is one more thing you need to think about before you can feel truly confident that you have a business strength that can be used as a basis for an aggressive marketing program. It is called the "Four-Point Test" and involves answers to the following four questions:

Figure 6.5
Tool Organizational Resource Inventory Worksheet

	Relevance	Rating	Notes
Physical Assets			
Production facilities			
Office facilities			
Financial Assets			
Equity in physical assets			
Cash reserves			
Lines of credit			
Loans			
Investment			
Personnel			
Executives			
Managers			
Operational/production			
Administrative			
Personnel recruitment			
Salaries & benefits			
Intellectual Property			
Patents & trademarks			
Know-how			
Innovation			

Figure 6.5 (*Continued*)

	Relevance	Rating	Notes
Organizational Processes			
Operational processes			
Organizational/Management processes			
Production capability			
Quality control			
Products & Services			
Product/service line #1			
Product/service line #2			
Product/service line #3			
Product/service line #4			
Brand equity			
New product/service development			
Customer support capability			
Technical support			
Problem resolution			
Customer base			
Size			
Location			
Segmentation			
Market share			

1. *Is it hard to copy?* You can be sure that if you have a significant competitive edge in the market, your competitors will try to copy it. You need to ask yourself how hard that would be and if you have the appropriate intellectual property protections (patents, trademarks, copyrights, etc.) in place to protect yourself.

   Remember that intellectual property protections are just a "first line of defense." Competitors will be working on finding ways to be just different enough to avoid potential action on your part. And some unscrupulous, deep-pocket competitors may even infringe on your rights, knowing that you might not have the financial resources to sue them and win.

2. *Is it durable?* If your strength is based on strong operational or managerial skills (e.g., marketing or new product development), that edge is likely to last. If, on the other hand, your strength is based on some new technological innovation or marketing approach, that strength may not last for long. We must continually be aware that the market and competitive landscapes are constantly changing.
3. *Is it competitively superior?* For some competency to be considered a competitive strength, it must be superior to similar strengths of key competitors. If you do the wrong thing extremely well, it doesn't help.
4. *Can it be trumped by different kind of competitive strengths?* Finally, it is important to recognize that "apples to apples" comparisons do not always work in business competition. Your hard-won competitive strength may be rendered obsolete or irrelevant if a competitor can find a new, better way to solve a problem. For example, your investments in efficient, state-of-the-art production facilities can be overcome by competitors who gain their price advantage by manufacturing in China.

WEAKNESSES

So far, I focused entirely on helping you to identify your real organizational strengths and have spent little time on weaknesses. That is because the definition of a competitive weakness is simple:

> Anything that the market requires and that is not a competitive strength is a weakness.

The Strengths Matrix

This discussion of strengths and weaknesses can be summarized as in Figure 6.6.

The cells in the matrix are shaded according to danger:

- *Dark shaded*: The dark shaded cells indicate where the truth about your actual business situation lies.
- *Diagonal stripes*: The cells with the diagonal strip pattern indicate areas where you may be wasting your time. We need to be continually aware that we cannot be tops in everything, and it can be a significant waste of time and resources to try. Your focus always should be on the things that actually make a difference.
- *Lightly shaded*: These are the danger zones. If you think you are strong in an important area, but are not, you will not spend the time and resources necessary to build your strengths in that area. This form of

Figure 6.6
Assessment of Strengths and Weaknesses

	Strengths I really have	Strengths I think I have, but don't	Weaknesses I think I have, but don't	Weaknesses I really have
Strengths I really need	**Real strengths**	**Arrogance**	**Virtual weaknesses**	**Real weaknesses**
Strengths I think I need, but don't	**Waste**	**Waste**	**Waste**	**Waste**

arrogance creates critical problems when the manager bases important strategic decisions on it. Similarly, believing you are weak in an area where you are not weak can result in critical organizational skills and resources not being utilized to their full effect.

Tool 6-D: Internal Factor Evaluation

The Internal Factor Evaluation (IFE) is similar to the External Factor Evaluation (EFE) except you put numbers to your strengths and weaknesses. The worksheet you will use is attached. A sample is presented in Figure 6.7.

Figure 6.7
Tool Internal Factor Evaluation

For each Identified factor:
How would you categorize it?
Major Opportunity = 4 Minor Threat = 2
Minor Opportunity = 3 Major Threat = 1
How important is that factor? Rate from 1-10, 10 being most important

External Factors		Factor Value (FV) (1-4)	Factor Weight (FW) (1-10)	Normalized Factor Weight (NW) =FW/TW	Weighted Factor =FV*NW
1					
2					
3					
4					
5					
6					
	Sums				

As was done with the External Factor Evaluation, the analysis itself is done in the following steps:

- *Step 1*: Select the most important internal factors you need to consider.
- *Step 2*: Assign a weight for each factor. Don't forget to convert the weights to percentages.
- *Step 3*: Assign a value for each factor. The internal equivalent to the scale recommended initially for the EFE would be:
  - 4 = Major strength
  - 3 = Minor strength
  - 2 = Minor weakness
  - 1 = Major weakness
- *Step 4*: Multiply and Sum
- *Step 5*: Validation: "Does this number make sense?"

Ted's Fish Market Example: Figure 6.8 shows how Mike Jameson completed the Internal Factor Evaluation for Ted's.

In general, this analysis shows decent business strength for Ted's. The one glaring weak point, however, is limited funds. He knows that he will need money for his planned expansion and that his bank is currently resistant.

Figure 6.8
Internal Factor Evaluation for Ted's Fish Market

	Internal Factors	Factor Value (FV) (1-4)	Factor Weight (FW) (1-10)	Normalized Factor Weight (NW) =FW/TW	Weighted Factor =FV*NW
1	Freshness	4	9	0.138	0.554
2	Prices	4	8	0.123	0.492
3	Service	4	7	0.108	0.431
4	Reputation	3	4	0.062	0.185
5	100 years old	3	2	0.031	0.092
6	Location	4	7	0.108	0.431
7	Historic Building	3	5	0.077	0.231
8	Not known outside area	2	5	0.077	0.154
9	Limited choices	1	5	0.077	0.077
10	Small facility	2	4	0.062	0.123
11	Limited money	1	9	0.138	0.138
		Sums	65	1.000	2.908

SUMMARY

- ☑ Assess your competencies thoroughly. You may have more than you think.
- ☑ Use the Four-Point Test for business strength.
- ☑ A weakness is anything that the marketplace demands and that is not your strength.

7

Identifying and Evaluating Your Competitors

Your strategic marketing plan must take into account the strengths and weaknesses of your competition, so you must know what they are doing and how they are faring.

Early in my career, I was called by the owner of a temporary help firm who had heard me speak at a conference. His business had once been very successful but now was beginning to fall on harder times. Although his sales had not actually dropped, new competitors had come into his market and were absorbing the rapid growth in demand for temporary help services in his city. His market share was falling and showed no signs of recovery.

My initial meetings with him indicated that he was "doing everything right."

- The people he provided were competent, experienced, and pleasant.
- If a customer was ever unhappy with any temp, he would immediately send a replacement.
- He was focusing his sales efforts on the larger users of temporary help. He said that the top 20 percent of temporary help users accounted for over 80 percent of all billings.
- He trained his salespeople to work only with the office managers of customers, because these people traditionally handled temporary staffing decisions.
- He rigorously adhered to all contractual agreements made to his customers and expected customers to do the same.

So, what was the problem? Why were these new companies doing so much better than he was?

My team and I developed a three-phase market research program to assess what the current market for temporary help was looking for. We began with a series of in-depth interviews with our client's largest customers. We then conducted a set of four focus groups. We finished with a set of over one hundred telephone interviews with a wide variety of temporary help users.

We were amazed by our results. The first thing that struck us was that there appeared to be almost no difference in the reputations of the five major suppliers of temporary help (our client included) among the heavy users (4 or more times per month) of temporary help. Everyone seemed pleased with their current vendor, and few had anything negative to say about any other vendor.

The surprise came when we looked at the lighter users of temporary help. Among this group, the reputation of the various firms coincided exactly with their current growth rates. Our client had an especially poor reputation among this segment of users.

When we looked further into this phenomenon, by going back to some of the people we had interviewed before, we discovered some very interesting things:

- Although among the larger users of temporary help, decisions regarding temporary help firms were made more formally by office managers, among the less frequent users, this decision was often made by a secretary, or even the receptionist, usually in response to some immediate need. Most often, if they did not already have a favorite firm, these people called the temporary help firm where the salesperson had been the nicest to them. My client's salespeople, on the other hand, had been trained to bypass receptionists and secretaries and to deal only with the office manager.
- The receptionists and junior secretaries in office buildings tended to know each other. They often met for coffee in the morning, for lunch, or for drinks after work. When a vendor did not treat one of them right, word quickly got around to everyone in the building.
- Receptionists and junior secretaries often rose in their careers by switching to higher paying jobs in other companies. When they moved, they would, of course, continue to use the temporary help vendors that they had already been successful with. And, they would tell their replacements about their experiences, too.
- The fast-growing firms were the ones that were focusing on these underserved customers. They were treating junior staff exceptionally well and insuring that the light users of temporary help were treated exceptionally well. (Sometimes, salespeople from these fast-growing temporary help firms would drop in just to provide some flowers or a candy bowl specifically for the receptionist.)
- The fast-growing firms were also very flexible with terms on contracts. They tried to make it as easy as possible for people to do business with them.

The impact of my client's determination to focus only on major users was obvious. Over time, his reputation was eroding as new, hungrier firms built their reputations working with smaller customers. Over just a few years, the entire competitive landscape had changed, and my client was still standing where he was years earlier!

There was a sad end to the story. My client's response to our findings was that "You don't know what you are talking about!" No significant changes were made. The company did not do well and was eventually bought out.

ASSESSING THE COMPETITION

The assessment of competition is one of the most common areas where businesspeople overly constrain their thinking. Competition consists of all of the different ways that your prospective customers, or any of your other business relationships, can meet their needs. The critical point to be made here is that businesspeople tend to look at competition only in terms of the products, services, and organizations that are very similar to what they offer themselves and ignore products, services, and organizations that may be very different but are, nonetheless, perceived as alternatives to customers. For example, Montgomery Ward knew how to compete with Sears and J.C. Penny, but not with Wal-Mart.

This chapter begins with an overview of the various types and levels of competition and how competitive environments operate. It then provides a competitive identification and evaluation methodology including:

- A process for identifying key competitors at various levels.
- An extensive set of questions to use when gathering information about competitors.
- Low-cost and no-cost methods for collecting accurate competitive information.

Defining Competition

Competition is simply the rivalry among organizations to obtain the same customers. If someone spends money at Company A rather than you, Company A is your competitor.

It has been my experience that entrepreneurs tend to define their competition too restrictively. For example, if someone has opened an Italian restaurant with banquet facilities, they would tend to see their competition as other Italian restaurants with banquet facilities.

The reality is that competition is widespread and exists on many levels.

Levels of Competition

There are four basic levels of competition:

- Level 1: Customer need: People perceive that they have many needs and these needs compete with each other for that person's money. Continuing with the Italian restaurant example, food and recreation compete with such things as housing, clothing, and savings for a piece of a family's income.

- Level 2: Industry competition: For any given need, there may be many industries that compete to fill it. For example, restaurants compete with grocery stores, convenience stores, farmers' markets, and "growing your own" as a source of food. In addition, restaurants compete with TV, movies, shopping, amusement venues, and a hundred other sources of recreation.
- Level 3: Product-line competition: Even within the restaurant industry, there is a wide range of basic choices: fast food, fine dining, Italian, Chinese, other ethnic, seafood, steak houses, and so on all competing for the dining customer.
- Level 4: Organizational or brand competition: Finally, we get to brand competition, where one Italian restaurant competes with the other Italian restaurants in the area.

Although there are technically four levels, in most cases we need only deal with the last two. The exception would be if you are trying to introduce a new type of product or service into the market. In this situation, it may be essential to identify and evaluate the Level 2 choices that customers might have.

For example, in my area, a new company has introduced prepackaged meals. It is a cross between a grocery store and a restaurant. You can go to this store and specify menus and quantities based on the foods they have prepared in their commercial kitchen. It is much like a restaurant, except that you can order several meals at a time and you can't eat there. You take the food home, put it in your refrigerator or freezer, and heat it when you are ready. Their prices are significantly higher than a grocery store's, but significantly lower than a restaurant's. The important thing here is that they compete with both.

IDENTIFYING COMPETITORS

With this hierarchy of competition in mind, you can now reevaluate who your competition is. As usual, I provided you a tool to do this.

Tool 7-A: Competition Inventory

A Competition Inventory simply needs three sheets of paper: one each for Levels 2, 3, and 4. Again, the goal here is to identify as many types of competition and specific competitors as possible. Remember that your marketplace, as a whole, has already done this: accurately or inaccurately. In other words, if a potential customer of yours is doing business with someone else rather than you, that other firm is your competition whether you think they should be or not!

Ted's Fish Market Example: Mike Jameson could have listed the following types of competition:

- Level 2 Competition: Food industry
  - Grocery stores: Stop & Shop, Safeway
  - Restaurants: Specifics vary with target market
  - Convenience stores

- Level 3 Competition: Seafood
  - Grocery store fish counters
  - Grocery store frozen fish
  - Seafood restaurants
- Level 4 Competition: Fish markets
  - Fin & Claw
  - Old Bay
  - Beacon Street
  - Woburn

INTENSITY OF COMPETITION

All competitive environments are not alike. Some industries and markets are full of competitors, whereas others have relatively few. In some industries and markets, the competition is very intense, whereas in others competitors pay little attention to each other. An important part of your strategic marketing approach will have to take these factors into consideration.

Number of Competitors

There are more competitors when:

- The opportunity is new: Whenever new opportunities open up, people jump in to fill that void. In these early stages, there are often more companies competing than the market can support. As the best (or biggest) firms come to dominate the market, less competitive firms will either close or refocus.
- The opportunity is large: If the opportunity is large and there are limits on the abilities of the largest, most successful, companies to fill all of that need, then there will be many firms competing for that opportunity. For example, larger cities have more restaurants, gas stations, lawyers, doctors, and business consultants than smaller cities do.
- It is easy to enter the market: If it is not difficult or expensive to get into a type of business, then lots of people will try.

Intensity of Competition

Competition among existing competitors is more intense when:

- Firms are highly committed to that market: This is the opposite of ease of entry. If a firm has a large investment in the industry or marketplace, or if leaving the marketplace will cause significant financial or reputational harm, it will fight hard to remain there.
- New products and technologies are introduced frequently: New products, services, and technologies can quickly change the competitive landscape.

Firms that want to remain in a fast-changing industry or market had better be prepared to invest heavily in product development and marketing.

- Low customer loyalty: If customers can be lured away by a better value, you can be sure that competitors will be trying to do so.
- There are significant economies of scale: If it is significantly more profitable to be large than small (i.e., businesses with relatively low variable costs as compared to fixed costs), then business will fight hard to gain sales volume and market share.

Researching Competitors

Now that you have identified your competition, your next task is to learn as much about them as you can.

The goal here is not to learn to be like them, although you will undoubtedly learn some valuable lessons in the process. Quite the contrary,

> Your goal is to identify ways in which you can create a distinct and powerful advantage over your competition.
>
> This is the essence of marketing!

Primary Sources of Information

There is usually a great deal of competitive information that you can gather yourself. Potential sources for competitive information include:

- Advertising: Perhaps the easiest method of gathering information about competitors is to collect and examine their advertising and other promotional materials, including their Web site (if they have one). Although this information will not provide an "inside" look at the company, it will tell you how that company wants to be perceived by the outside world and, to a large extent, how the firm perceives itself.
- Visiting: If you can pull this off without misrepresenting yourself, seeing what your competitors have and do is very important. This is especially the case where you are offering products or services to the general public. For example, it is easy to visit a competitive retail store or restaurant.
- Customers: Your customer, particularly the loyal ones, can be an invaluable source of information. Ask them about any experiences they or their friends may have had with competitive firms and what the reputation of those firms might be in the marketplace. Just be careful not to ask them to do anything unethical to obtain information for you.
- Your sales force: If you have salespeople out calling on customers, they will run into competitive situations. Ask your salespeople to gather as much information as they can about the competition they face on a sale and share that information with you.
- Suppliers: If you are buying products or services from a supplier that also deals with one or more of your competitors, they may be willing to share some information with you, particularly if they are trying to sell you additional products and services. Just remember that if they will

tell you something about a competitor, they will most likely be willing to share information about you too.

- Competitors' products: If it is feasible to do so, buy samples of your competitors' products and test them thoroughly yourself.
- Trade shows: If you plan to go to trade shows as a part of your marketing strategy (more about this in later chapters), take the time to check out those of your competitors who are also attending the show.

Secondary Sources of Information

And there are yet more sources for finding useful knowledge:

- Web searches: One of the easiest things you can do is to Google (or Yahoo or Ask) your competition. Search on your industry, your particular product/service types, and specific competitor names.
- Internet newsgroups and blogs: There are newsgroups and blogs about almost any subject you can think of (and a lot that will surprise you). Try to find newsgroups and sensible blogs about your industry, your product types, and your specific competitors.
- Newspapers, magazines, and journals: Every day hundreds of business-related articles appear in newspapers, news magazines, business magazines, and academic journals. Subjects include market analyses, industry analyses, economic forecasts, and company profiles. Fortunately, there are two excellent databases that are available to find this information:
  - Business Source Premier: This database is a product of EBSCO Publishing and contains the full text of articles in over 2,300 publications going back to 1965. In addition, Business Source Premier contains many
    - Market research reports
    - Industry reports
    - Country reports
    - Company profiles
    - SWOT Analyses
  - Proquest Research Library: This database is more general than Business Source Premier but still covers over 3,800 newspapers, magazines, and academic journals n a wide range of subjects. I have found their business coverage to be particularly good.
- Fortunately, these databases are generally available for free through your local public library or university. I strongly recommend a visit with a skilled reference librarian before you start.
- Data services:
  - Dun & Bradstreet Online: Provides short reports on approximately 10 million American businesses, including many privately held companies.
  - Lexis-Nexis: This powerful database provides business information including business and financial news, U.S. and international company financial information, market research, industry reports, and actual

SEC filings. Financial information covered includes that available through Hoovers and Standard & Poor.
  - Hoover's Online: Provides income and balance sheet numbers for public companies.

- These databases may also be available for free through your local public library, college or university.
- Trade associations: Trade associations are one of the most important ways in which the firms in a given industry work together to promote and protect that industry.
- The *Encyclopedia of Associations* (once again, check your local library or college) cites over 135,000 nonprofit membership organizations worldwide, including more than 22,200 national associations, 22,300 international associations, and more than 115,000 U.S. local or regional associations. The *Encyclopedia of Associations* database provides addresses and descriptions of professional societies, trade associations, labor unions, cultural and religious organizations, fan clubs, and other groups of all types. The larger trade associations often have research divisions studying industry trends and trade magazines with articles and profiles of interest. A hint: Trade magazines usually solicit advertisements. The "media kit" they provide to potential advertisers often contains a clear and thorough analysis of the industry the association represents. These media kits can sometimes even be downloaded from the Internet.
- Consultants: There are companies and individuals that specialize in gathering competitive information. Two of the best known are Fuld & Company (www.Fuld.com) and marketresearch.com, although there may be excellent consultants in your regional area.

COMPETITIVE ANALYSIS TOOLS

There are two more tools that I would like to share with you: the 555 Matrix and the Competitive Profile Matrix.

Tool 7-B: The 555 Matrix

I designed the 555 Matrix several years ago as a business research and analysis tool that I could use in a casual conversation and that would:

- Produce immediate, powerful results.
- Be easy to learn and administer.
- Require only pencil and paper.

The idea was to have a tool that would enable the user to quickly grasp someone's view of their competitive situation and would also be very easy to understand and nonthreatening. Figure 7.1 shows what it looks like:

Start your analysis by identifying what you believe to be your four most critical competitors. You and these four constitute the five columns of the matrix.

Figure 7.1
The 555 Matrix

	You	Competitor A	Competitor B	Competitor C	Competitor D
Dif 1					
Dif 2					
Dif 3					
Dif 4					
Dif 5					
Total					

Next, identify what you believe to be the five most important factors that differentiate among you and your competitors in the minds of customers. Remember that when it comes to marketing, it's the customers' beliefs, whether true or not, that determine their purchasing behavior.

Rate each company on a scale of 1 to 5 (low to high) for each factor. It is OK if you give the same score to more than one company.

Then total the ratings to get a rough gauge of competitive strength.

Finally, step back and ask yourself: "Does this make sense?" If it does, you have something to work with. If not, review your selections for competitors and differentiators as well as your ratings.

Ted's Fish Market Example: Here is an example of what the completed matrix might look like if were being done for Ted's Fish Market in New England. Review Figure 7.2.

Figure 7.2
555 Matrix for Ted's Fish Market

	Ted's	Fin & Claw	Old Bay	Beacon St.	Woburn
Freshness	5	3	5	3	5
Choice	3	3	4	5	2
Price	4	2	4	3	5
Service	4	5	2	5	2
Reputation	4	2	4	5	3
	20	15	19	21	17

If we assume that Ted is reasonably accurate in his assessments, The Beacon Street Market is his strongest competitor.

But, more can be learned. If Beacon Street's areas of strength are, in fact, choice and service, that is good news for Ted. These strengths are relatively easily copied, whereas Ted's advantage of freshness, dependent on his excellent relationship with the actual fishermen, is much harder to duplicate.

Although it is certainly possible to self-administer this tool, it actually works better, on you, if someone else does it. You can also use it to gather information from friends, suppliers, and customers.

Tool 7-C: Competitive Profile Matrix

The Competitive Profile Matrix (Figure 7.3) looks like a cross between the EFE and the 555 Matrix. It is much more detailed and rigorous than a 555 Matrix and allows for the careful consideration of key differentiating factors.

The steps in completing this form are very similar to the IFE and EFE I have described previously:

- Step 1: Select the most important factors you need to consider. These should be the factors that most clearly differentiate you and your competitors in the minds of the marketplace.
- Step 2: Assign a weight for each factor. Don't forget to convert the weights to percentages.
- Step 3: Assign a value for each factor to yourself and each of your competitors. Use the same four-point scale we used for the Internal Factor Evaluation (IFE):
    - 4 = Major strength
    - 3 = Minor strength
    - 2 = Minor weakness
    - 1 = Major weakness
- Step 4: Multiply and sum
- Step 5: Validation. Ask yourself: "Does this number make sense?" If something does not look or feel right to you, go back and reassess whether you have
    - Chosen the right competitors
    - Selected the most important differentiators
    - Accurately assessed yourself and each selected competitor
    - Done the arithmetic correctly.

Ted's Fish Market Example: An example of a completed Competitive Profile Matrix for Ted's is shown in Figure 7.4.

Figure 7.3
The Competitive Profile Matrix

			Your Company		Competitor 1		Competitor 2		Competitor 3	
Evaluation Factors	Factor Weight (1-10)	Normalized Factor Weight	Factor Value (1-4)	Weighted Factor	Factor Value (1-4)	Weighted Factor	Factor Value (1-4)	Weighted Factor	Factor Value (1-4)	Weighted Factor
1										
2										
3										
4										
5										
6										
Totals										

For each Identified Factor:

How would you categorize it?

Major Strength = 4 Minor Strength = 3 Minor Weakness = 2 Major Weakness = 1

How important is that factor? Rate from 1-10, 10 being most important

Figure 7.4
Competitive Profile Matrix for Ted's Fish Market

	Evaluation Factors	Factor Weight (1-10)	Normalized Factor Weight	Ted's Factor Value (1-4)	Ted's Weighted Factor	Old Bay Factor Value (1-4)	Old Bay Weighted Factor	Beacon St. Factor Value (1-4)	Beacon St. Weighted Factor	Woburn Factor Value (1-4)	Woburn Weighted Factor
1	Freshness	8	0.216	4	0.865	4	0.865	3	0.649	4	0.865
2	Choice	6	0.162	3	0.486	4	0.649	4	0.649	3	0.486
3	Price	7	0.189	4	0.757	4	0.757	3	0.568	4	0.757
4	Service	8	0.216	4	0.865	2	0.432	4	0.865	2	0.432
5	Reputation	5	0.135	3	0.405	2	0.270	4	0.541	3	0.405
6	Size	3	0.081	2	0.162	4	0.324	3	0.243	2	0.162
		Total Weight	Total NW		Total Score		Total Score		Total Score		Total Score
		37	1.000		3.541		3.297		3.514		3.108

For each Identified Factor:
How would you categorize it?
Major Strength = 4 Minor Weakness = 2
Minor Strength = 3 Major Weakness = 1
How important is that factor? Rate from 1-10, 10 being most important

SUMMARY

- ☑ You probably have more competition than you think.
- ☑ There are several levels of competition.
- ☑ The intensity of your competitive environment depends on the number of competitors and how hard each is fighting for success.
- ☑ There are many free sources of competitive information that you can get access to.
- ☑ Use the 555 Matrix as a starting point.

8

Positioning Your Product or Service

Positioning is about how your product or service is perceived in the mind of the consumer and is the focus of this chapter.

Selling Smelly Stuff home heating oil is not the most exciting product I have ever marketed. It smells bad, costs a lot, is flammable, and sits in large tanks in basements. Several years ago, I had a client who wanted to increase his sales of home heating oil in a neighboring county. He had the predominant market share in the county in which he was located but was having a hard time achieving similar results in the next county over.

At that point in time, home heating oil was sold as annual contracts, including the fuel itself, along with a furnace inspection and repair contract. Traditionally, contractors won new contracts through referral from real estate agents. The assumption was that once a customer selected a contractor, that customer remained with that contractor. Therefore, you had to get a customer right at the time they bought their house or you lost your chance. As a result, home heating oil salespeople spent most of their time building relationships in the real estate community.

Because the sales approach was based on the presumption you needed referrals from real estate agents, we decided to begin our efforts by questioning that assumption. We then came up with four primary reasons why people would get a new heating oil contract:

1. Moving from a home with oil heat to another home with oil heat.
2. Moving from a home without oil heat to a home with oil heat.
3. Changing contractors to get a lower price.
4. Changing contractors because they were unhappy.

Numbers 1 and 2 were where the entire focus of attention of most contractors' marketing efforts (including my client's) was placed.

The price leader in the county was a national firm that had enough financial resources to offer very low prices for the first-year contracts, giving up the first-year's profit on the expectation of long-term commitment. My client was not willing to engage in a price war with a much richer firm.

No one at all was focusing on unhappy customers.

I went to the courthouse to look at the housing records for the county. Fortunately, heating system was one of the housing factors that county was tracking. I found something remarkable. Although there were many homes bought and sold each year in the county, homes with oil heat were mostly older homes and turned over quite rarely. In fact, we would have had to secure contracts with almost all of people buying these older homes if we were going to make our client's goals!

In other words, despite the common knowledge that the way to sell oil heat contracts was to focus on people buying these homes, that market was far smaller than anyone thought.

So we went after people who were unhappy with their present contractors and ended up tapping into a need we initially did not know existed. There were a lot more dissatisfied customers of our competitors than we ever expected. In the minds of the consumer, the company soon became known as the "high-quality" oil heat contractor. The result was a threefold increase in sales for our client.

LEARNING AND APPLYING WHAT MAKES YOU SPECIAL

Everyone wants to be special. Entrepreneurs want to be extra special. We know we have great products and great services. If only the marketplace knew, we'd be swamped with customers.

Despite the fact that everyone believes themselves to be special, only some achieve great success. The rest wonder what happened, what the secret is.

The secret is, in fact quite simple. No matter how wonderful your product or service really is, the opinion of the marketplace is all that matters!

The marketplace is crowded with companies, many of which, like you, have excellent products or services. All these companies are marketing their brains out trying to get attention, trying to get their message out. Your job, therefore, is to create a compelling reason why someone out there should pay attention to you, rather than all of the rest of the noise out there.

But people will not pay attention to you because you have a slick logo and a catchy motto. They will pay attention because you:

1. Offer something that is distinctly new and interesting, and, at the same time,
2. Reflect their prevailing beliefs.

Limitations of Marketing

Marketing is nowhere near as powerful as many people think. Organizations spend millions of dollars and employ the most creative marketing talent trying to get us to stop littering, not drink and drive, and support our local Public Broadcasting Stations (PBS), but there are still many litterers, drunk drivers, and only a small minority support PBS. Other products, like Starbucks, seem to succeed seemingly with no effort at all.

Positioning, how the buyer perceives the product or service, is often the key to marketing success. Yet despite the simplicity of the concept, positioning is one of the most talked about and least understood concepts in marketing. That is because people often use two, contradictory definitions of positioning:

1. How the marketplace actually perceives your products, and
2. How you would like the marketplace to perceive your products.

In the first case "position" is most often used as a noun. The sentence: "This is my market position," usually means "This is how the marketplace perceives my products or services."

In the second case, "position" is used as a verb. The sentence "I position my product as the most cost-effective alternative" means that is how I want the marketplace to perceive my product. I will refer to #1 as your true position and #2 as your intended position.

The ideal situation is for #1 and #2 to be the same. It doesn't always happen that way, however. Although an organization can influence its market position in the minds of its marketplace, it cannot simply choose it. With that in mind, this chapter provides practical methods for:

- Determining your true position in the context of the competitive information gathered
- Evaluating the strength of that position
- Selecting (if desirable) an improved intended position to set as a goal.

RIES AND TROUT

In their 1981 book *Positioning: The Battle for Your Mind* (McGraw-Hill, 2000) Al Ries and Jack Trout permanently changed the ways marketers think about their craft. Their contribution is critical, so I review the key points they made.

The Need to Be Right

The sheer quantity of information that people must sift through continues to grow more rapidly than most people ever imagined. Even writing in 1981, before the worldwide adoption of the Internet and the wide-spread adoption of cable TV, Ries and Trout argued that the amount of information, especially marketing information, that people were presented with was far greater than their capacity to process. Their only choice was to filter almost all of it out. In particular, people filter out what is irrelevant to them and what contradicts what they think they already know. (More about this in Chapter 10.)

The idea that people filter out what they do not already agree with may be counterintuitive to many people, even many marketers. It seems reasonable to think that people will pay attention to things that are new and exciting: products, services, and ideas that provide significantly better ways of achieving their needs and goals than they had before. Yes, it is reasonable. It just doesn't work that way.

No one likes to be wrong. People will hold onto their beliefs with an incredible tenacity. We all know how risky it is to try to engage people in discussions of religion and politics. The reason is that those subjects are about belief systems, and people are extremely reluctant to entertain the possibility that they are wrong, especially about core beliefs. Just try to convince even your closest friends to change their support of a candidate you don't like.

We do the same with the products and services we buy. Most people choose a certain product and stick with it. There are just too many products out there for people to continually redecide. Imagine how long it would take you to go to the grocery store if you had to make decisions about each brand of soup, juice, paper towels, and so on. If you have ever had to shop in a foreign country, you know what I am saying. And once those decisions are made, people do not want to make them again. There is just too much else to do. As a result, when a new ad appears touting "new," or "revolutionary," or "unique," it mostly falls on deaf ears. That information does not "compute." It does not agree with what we already know, and once a mind is made up, it is almost impossible to change it.

The Solution: Be a New Leader

The solution is to offer a category of product that people have not decided upon. In other words, redefine what you do so that you can be seen as the first and best at it.

People remember firsts. Who was the first president? Who was the second? Who was the first person to walk on the moon? Who was the second?

Now a trick question: Who was the first person to introduce the phrase "survival of the fittest?" No, it was not Charles Darwin. It was Herbert Spencer. The phrase was not even used by Darwin until the fifth edition of his book *Origin of Species*, and, even then, he cited Spencer.

The point is people remember who becomes known as the first, rather than who really is the first.

For example, in the home heating oil case presented in this chapter, we promoted this idea to unhappy customers: If anyone ever ran out of home heating oil, no matter whose customer it was, our client would be there within one hour to fill the tank no matter, including nights and holidays. The truth was that any heating oil contractor in town would do the same thing, but no one actually said so. We were the first to make that powerful claim. We created a new category of heating oil providers based on reliability, and our client quickly became known as the most reliable provider in the area.

The key to being a successful product/service leader is to create a new category in which you are seen and acknowledged to be the first and best (even if, in reality, you might not be). If you are trying to convince someone that your brand is better, then you have already chosen a category in which there are other brands and, therefore, preexisting preferences and ideas. Better to introduce a new type of product or service where people have not already made up their minds.

Successful examples include:

- Starbucks: Upscale coffee shops
- Wal-Mart: Large stores in small towns
- Target: Upscale discount stores
- iPod: Small, programmable music player

DEFINING YOUR MARKET POSITION

Your goal is to have a true position in the marketplace that will:

- Accurately reflect your actual distinctive competencies and differential advantage
- Focus on unserved or underserved market segments
- Be achievable given current resources
- Be sustainable over the longer term
- Be defensible in the face of competitive response.

Any attempt at establishing a new market position must reflect the truth about the competitive environment as seen by consumers in that marketplace. You can't just make up a position, advertise the daylights out of it, and expect people to believe it. This requires that you have as good a sense as possible about the competitive environment in which you operate.

A powerful tool for analyzing the competitive information you gathered (in Chapter 7) in terms of market positions is the Perceptual Map.

Tool 8-A: The Perceptual Map

The Perceptual Map is used by marketers to assess the positioning (true or intended) of a product or company. A generic Perceptual Map is shown in Figure 8.1.

Now that you are familiar with both the 555 Matrix and the Competitive Profile Matrix, doing a Perceptual Map should be pretty straightforward.

There are four steps to using the Perceptual Map:

- Step 1: Select two of the key factors that the marketplace uses to differentiate among competitors.
- Step 2: Evaluate each of your important competitors along these two dimensions.
- Step 3: Display the results in a two-dimensional grid.
- Step 4: Look for patterns, especially open spaces in the grid.

To illustrate, let's use the data we have already collected for Ted's Fish Market. To refresh your memory, Figure 8.2 shows Ted's 555 Matrix.

Figure 8.1
Generic Perceptual Map

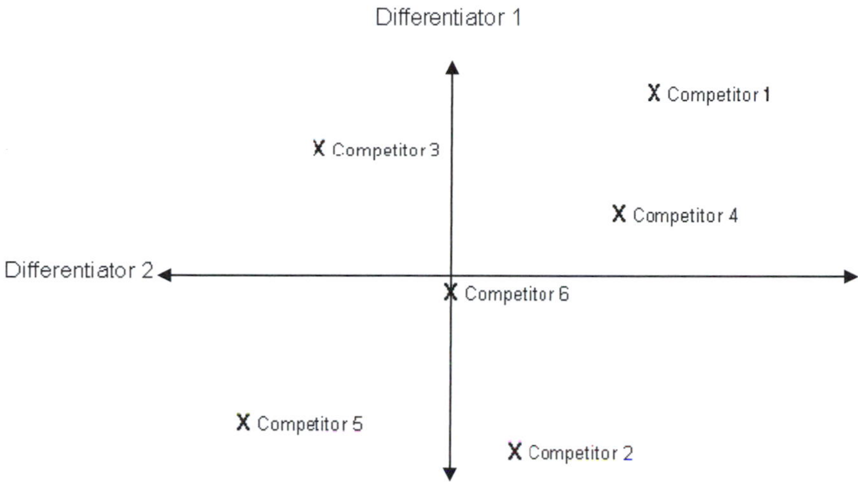

For purposes of illustration, I have chosen Price and Service as the key differentiating factors. The factors Freshness and Choice are the kinds of issues that customers always want more of. In other words, there is no opportunity to reposition Ted's by offering less of one of them. On the other hand, customers may well be willing to accept less service if they get to pay less.

The perceptual map of Price against Service for Ted's would look like Figure 8.3.

Figure 8.2
555 Matrix for Ted's Fish Market

	Ted's	Fin & Claw	Old Bay	Beacon St.	Woburn
Freshness	5	3	5	3	5
Choice	3	3	4	5	2
Price	4	2	4	3	5
Service	4	5	2	5	2
Reputation	4	2	4	5	3
	20	15	19	21	17

Figure 8.3
A Perceptual Map for Ted's Fish Market

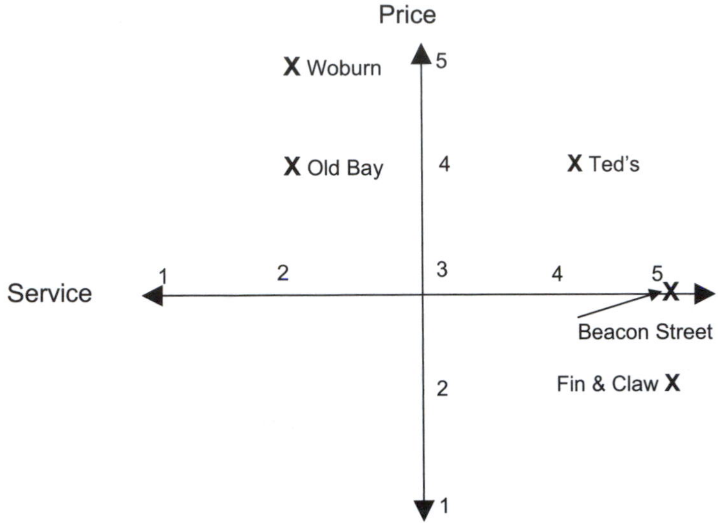

From this perspective, Ted's appears to be in pretty good shape. It is the only one among the competitors to be in positive territory on both price and service. However, if Ted's could improve its service to at least the standard of Beacon Street and Fin & Claw, it could make its position as the best-price service mix even more solid. Then it would be in a much better situation than either of those two competitors. They could no longer claim the service advantage and would have to lower prices to match Ted.

The problem, of course, comes in changing the mind of the consumer. If Beacon Street and Fin & Claw have the reputation of great service, and the marketplace accepts it, it will be hard for Ted's to start claiming the same thing. "Me too" does not work very well. Ted's would have to find some specific aspect of service in which the other two were weak (e.g., home delivery, recipe advice, prepackaged dinners), become first in claiming those services, and use those services to bolster its claims.

If Necessary, Establish a New Intended Market Position

Once you know what your true position is, you get to decide whether you like it or not and, if not, where your new intended market position should be.

If you decide to try to change your market position, do not do so based on hope or ego. Consumers will always go with your true position, not your intended position. Therefore, your intended position has to be based on truth and has to be focused on an underserved market segment that you can be best in:

- *Positioning tactics*: There are many tactical options open to you if you choose to position a new product or reposition an existing one. Some of the choices are listed below. It is not necessary to choose just one. In many ways, the more specifically you position your products and services, the better you will succeed. There are six tactics for positioning a product based upon whether you use benefits, uses, features, niches, competitors, or values and price.
- *Positioning based on the benefits of your product or service*: "With our product, you will ..." This is the cleanest positioning strategy. It goes straight for creating the anticipation of a valued experience. The home cleaning company Merry Maids uses the slogan "Relax, It's Done." Note that there is nothing in that slogan about how much better than their competition they are, or even about what they do. It is all about the benefit, relaxation, that the customer will receive by using them.
- *Positioning based on the specific uses of your product or service*: "With our product, you can ..." One way to position your product is to focus on a specific use or set of uses that are not being featured by your competition. Arm & Hammer Baking Soda was originally used for baking. As the demand for baking soda in grocery stores declined, Arm & Hammer found a new use for its product—deodorizing refrigerators—and sales took off.
- *Positioning based on product features and attributes*: "Our product has/can ..." Here the positioning is based on having unique product features, and, therefore, unique product benefits. A good example here is the Select Comfort Sleep Number® bed. They were the first in the marketplace with a bed where the firmness on each side of the bed was independently adjustable.
- *Positioning toward market niches*: "Our products are for ..." The idea here is to become the leading provider of your product to a clearly identified group. Tylenol has thirty-nine versions of its product, not counting size and packaging differences. These versions most often relate to specific types of pain. For example, Tylenol has specific product to use for menstrual pain, arthritis pain, allergy pain, colds, and congestion. Interestingly, the active ingredients in Tylenol 8-Hour are exactly the same as in Tylenol Arthritis Pain. The difference is the market positioning.
- *Some clothing stores are also excellent at positioning*: Abercrombie & Fitch, a century-old company that began as a safari outfitter, successfully repositioned itself as the teenage and preteen fashion mecca. Similarly Chico's has become highly successful as a preferred store for professional women who want to look feminine.
- *Positioning relative to competitors*: "Our products are like...." This is an interesting strategy where you compare yourself directly to a competitor in a way that highlights your differences. Perhaps the most famous of these were the Avis "We're Number 2" campaign and the 7-Up "The Uncola" campaign.
- *Positioning in terms of value/price*: "Our products cost..." Major grocery store and drug store chains have "house brands." These are positioned specifically to be lower-cost alternatives to specific national brands.

Take mouthwashes, for example. For each major brand, for example, Listerine, Scope, there is usually a house brand with the same basic ingredients, the same color, and the same shaped bottle. And they are placed on the shelf right next to the national brands.

FOUR POSITIONING PITFALLS

There are four major mistakes people make when attempting to position or reposition their products: underpositioning, overpositioning, confused positioning, and doubtful positioning.

Underpositioning

"Underpositioning" means that you have not been clear or specific enough about where you stand. As a result, the marketplace does not know what your brand stands for, and you become vulnerable to competitors who are more effectively positioned.

The large American department stores had this problem. Although the retail market was relatively stable, giants such as Sears and Montgomery Ward could grow continually larger, while regional department store chains found secure followings in their metropolitan areas. Wal-Mart, along with Best Buy, Target, and a plethora of specifically targeted clothing stores (e.g., Gap, Old Navy) changed the game. Wal-Mart grew by establishing and ruthlessly maintaining an "everyday low price" strategy and by targeting the nonmetropolitan areas that the larger stores believed could not support a department store. Although the big chains continued to try to be everything to everybody, Wal-Mart stuck to its position as the low price leader and thrived.

Overpositioning

Overpositioning is when you are so well known for one specific thing that you cannot move successfully into other areas. One of the most famous cases was Xerox's failed attempt in the 1970s to get into the computer business. Xerox was for copying, not computing. A more close-to-home example was the failure of A-1 Chicken Sauce. A-1 was clearly the leader in steak sauces and was unable to extend that to include chicken. They could not move from steak sauce to "meat" sauce.

Confused Positioning

Confused positioning is an attempt to make your brand mean more than one thing. For example, over the past twenty years or so, American automobile companies have tried to introduce models of almost every type for almost every brand. As a result, it has become increasingly harder for customers to know what a particular brand means.

Currently, Chevrolet offers five different kinds of cars, three different passenger trucks, and five different SUVs, with pricing ranging from around $11,000 for an Aveo, to about $80,000 for a loaded Corvette. Is Chevrolet a big car or a small car? Is it an economy car or a performance car? Are they expensive or inexpensive? So, what does "Chevrolet" mean? At one time Chevrolet meant a solid American car. But that is not even true anymore because the Aveo is made in Korea by Daewoo, a GM subsidiary.

Doubtful Positioning

Doubtful positioning is trying to establish a new market position that is so far from your current position that the marketplace will just not accept it. For example, Lifesavers failed with chewing gum. Another example is the twice failed attempt by Cadillac to introduce a small luxury car to compete with BMW. Cadillac just does not mean "small" in the mind of the American public.

BRANDING

Branding is conceptually easy to define, but many people have a hard time with it anyway. Branding is putting a clear, memorable label on your market position. The purpose of a brand is to lock in your market position and remind the customer of who you are and what you stand for. A trademark is the legal term for the image (i.e., logo or script) that you use to identify your brand.

Brands should have four characteristics:

- Easy to say
- Easy to spell
- Easy to read
- Easy to remember

Because your brand is how people remember who you are, it is critical that you treat your brand as a valuable asset to be developed and nurtured, just like our personal reputation. If you do things well, over time you will develop what is called "brand equity." In other words, your brand, itself, comes to have value because of what it calls forth in the minds of consumers.

But this is where too many entrepreneurs get into trouble. The more your brand develops a reputation and becomes valuable to you, the more what your brand represents becomes fixed in the minds of consumers. Therefore, you can impeach that brand equity by:

- Using the brand on products or services that are too far afield from what people currently think the brand stands for.
- Introducing shoddy product or services and eroding the respect your brand has.
- Letting others use your brand (e.g., franchising) without tight controls on what they can and cannot do.

SUMMARY

- ☑ Positioning yourself is essential to marketing success.
- ☑ It is hard to change people's mind.
- ☑ Leverage what people already believe to make ourselves unique.
- ☑ It is better to be the biggest fish in a smaller pond than one more fish in a large pond.
- ☑ Use the Perceptual Map to assess your real and intended positions in the marketplace.
- ☑ There are many positioning choices.
- ☑ Avoid the four positioning pitfalls.
- ☑ Branding can lock your position into the minds of consumers.

9

Pricing Your Products and Services

Pricing is perhaps the most misunderstood and least well planned aspect of marketing. We tend to spend a great deal of time, energy, and money developing products and promoting them to the marketplace. Then, when it comes time to decide what to ask them to pay for the product, we get confused.

In the seminar during which we introduced the 555 Matrix, a woman volunteered to be the first "guinea pig" to try out this new tool. She had taken over running a document translation company that her parents had started years earlier.

Her issue was that she wanted to grow her business but did not have the financial resources to do so. She was trying to keep her prices "competitive" and, despite significant revenue, did not have much net profit. She was looking for some very inexpensive ways that she could use to promote her business.

When we did the 555 Matrix with her, something jumped out. She claimed to be the price leader and the quality leader in her regional market. I pointed out that, if this were true, she was probably either doing too much or charging too little. Either way, her customers were probably getting a bargain.

Because she did dot have the funds to retain me as a consultant, one of my graduate student teams took on her company as a class project. The results of their work confirmed what we had discussed earlier. Her customers were very happy with her company's work. There were even a number of extra services (e.g., delivery of documents) that she performed without the usual extra charges.

She was intending to provide the best possible service she could to her customers, and that is a good thing. However, she did not believe that her customers were willing to pay for the extraordinary quality and service she provided. She was afraid that if she raised prices, customers would desert her and go to the lower-priced alternatives. We pointed out to her that this was not logical.

- If her customers did not care about her exceptional quality and service, but only cared about price, she could increase her profit by cutting out some of these "frills."
- If her customers cared about her service, they would not desert her for a firm providing a lower level of service and quality just to save money.

In other words, there was no real point to her trying to have it both ways. She had happy customers, but no money and no resources to grow the business. What was the point?

We recommended to her that she begin to raise her prices, slowly at first, and see what happened. The results were excellent. Her profits started to rise, and few customers left. She finally had the resources to start growing.

GETTING THE ECONOMICS RIGHT

Put simply, pricing is where we get back the value that we have provided through our products and services.

The key pricing question is this: "What is the value that our customers get from our products and services?" In other words, it is not our costs but their benefits that should determine price. If our costs are less than that value, we should be able to reap a profit. Otherwise, we will incur a loss.

Of course, in the real world, it is not quite this simple. In this chapter, I outline the specific considerations that an entrepreneur should have in mind when developing pricing.

EXTERNAL CONSIDERATIONS IN SETTING PRICES

When we go about setting prices, there are external and internal factors that must be considered.

The major external issues you must consider are:

- What the market will bear.
- Price elasticity of demand.
- Perceived value relative to competition.
- Nonmonetary aspects of price (convenience, service, buying experience, availability, etc.).

What the Market Will Bear

This common phrase reflects the basic understanding of the concept of customer value. Customers will not pay more for a product or service than the monetarily equivalent value they place on the benefits derived from that product or service. At the same time, not everyone will perceive or experience the same benefits. So it is difficult to base pricing on this alone.

Price Elasticity of Demand

"Price elasticity of demand" is a fancy term for the fact that the more you raise the price, the less people will buy. In other words, if the price is higher, only the people who will derive benefit greater than the cost increase will buy. Although if the price is less, more people may buy because there is a lower threshold before the value of the benefit is applied.

Economists graph this phenomenon simply as in Figure 9.1.

Implications of Price Elasticity—Inelastic Demand

Price elasticity is measured as the percentage change in revenue as the result of a percentage change in price. For example, suppose you provide a software program that sells for $200. At that price, you can sell 500 per month. Now, you decide to raise your price to $250 each, a 25 percent increase, and you notice that sales drop to 400 per month, a 20 percent drop. The price elasticity would be measured as the change in demand, divided by the change in price. The price elasticity would be calculated as 20/25 or 0.8.

In this case, the demand for your product is somewhat inelastic, that is, it is less than 1.0. In other words, demand does not drop off by as much as you have increased your price. This means that your profits will be higher with the higher price and the lower volume. Your revenue has not changed (at both price levels, you are receiving $100,000 per month in revenue), but your volume is lower, so you do not incur the variable costs of production, delivery, and customer support for 100 more units a month. The implication here, is that if demand for your product is inelastic (i.e., less than 1.0), raising your prices will increase your profit.

Price Elasticity and Revenue

If demand for your product is elastic (i.e., greater than 1.0), sales will increase disproportionately to a price cut.

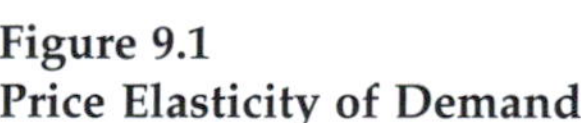

Figure 9.1
Price Elasticity of Demand

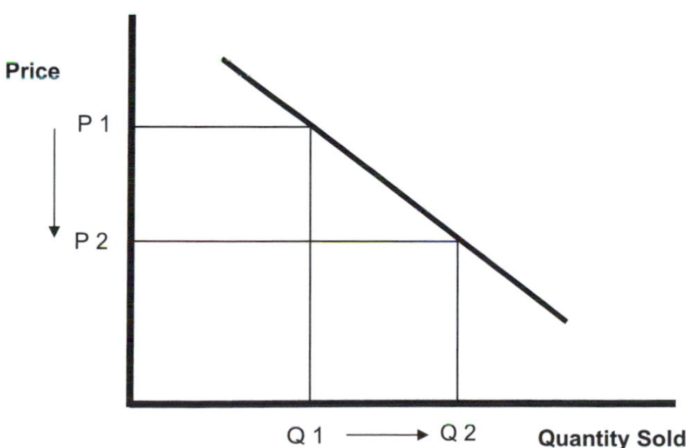

Suppose this time, that you have a buffet restaurant. Your basic lunch buffet is $10, and you have a sales volume of about 6,000 per month (200 people per day), yielding a sales volume of $60,000 per month. As a test, you decide to lower your lunch prices by $1 or 10 percent and discover that 250 people per day (7,500 people per month or a 25 percent increase) start coming to your restaurant. The price elasticity in this case is 2.5 (25 percent revenue increase divided by a 10 percent price decrease). Your monthly sales volume has now increased to $67,500. In other words, when price is elastic, a decrease in price produces an increase in revenue. Similarly, an increase in price will result in a decrease in revenue.

Price Elasticity and Profit

In considering the implications of a price change, it is very important that we recognize that elasticity measures revenue change, not profit change. Clearly, if we increase prices in an inelastic situation revenue will increase as volume drops. Because we no longer will incur the variable costs of production and delivery, profits will grow.

The situation is not so clear in elastic situations. If we are lowering price to increase revenue, we will also be increasing costs. This cost increase will reduce, or perhaps even eliminate, the benefit of the revenue increase.

For example, we can go back to the buffet restaurant. Suppose it costs you $5 to provide the food and drink for each customer. At $10 each, you have a gross profit of $5 each. However, if you do not change your variable costs (e.g., by reducing the buffet selections), a price reduction of $1 would reduce your gross profit to $4 per customer. Is this worth doing? Here are the calculations shown on a monthly basis:

At $10 per customer

Number of customers	6,000
Revenue	$60,000
Variable costs ($5 each)	$30,000
Gross profit	$30,000

At $9 per customer

Number of customers	7,500
Revenue	$67,500
Variable costs ($5 each)	$37,500
Gross profit	$30,000
Percent increase in gross profit	0.0%

In this situation, you have no increase in profit, despite a 20 percent increase in the number of customers. Is it worth doing?

Estimating Price Elasticity

The problem, of course, is estimating the price elasticity for your product or service before you make a price change. This is not easy to do. In particular, you cannot use the results of a temporary price cut, because some regular customer will stock up at the lower price because they know the price is going back up.

In highly competitive environments where the customer has many choices and prices are publicly known, product will tend to be highly elastic. Customers will quickly shift to less expensive alternatives. On the other hand, if products are essential and if there is little or no competition, demand will be inelastic and customers will (albeit resentfully) pay whatever the provider demands. Examples are cable television and refreshments at sporting events.

Before you alter your prices to generate increased revenue or profit, it is important to think through the situation and understand as well as you can what your competitive situation is. Then, before you act, look at some of the potential scenarios using a break-even analysis, discussed below. Also, if you do make a price change, give it some time before you evaluate the results. When you change your pricing, there will be an adjustment period during which customers and competitors learn about your new prices and decide how to react.

Backwards Elasticity

There are two situations where the common sense of price elasticity of demand does not apply and that is when price, itself, becomes a value. This situation applies to some kinds of luxury goods (e.g., cars, boats, vacation homes, jewelry, etc.) where the customer wants to believe that they have purchased "the best." In these cases, raising prices may actually increase demand. The other situation is speculative markets. For example, if someone is buying a house in a market where housing prices are going up, they may want buy the most expensive house they can afford to get the greater appreciation on that greater investment.

Perceived Value Relative to Competition

Just as the marketplace will develop perceptions (accurate or not) of the positions various products have in that marketplace, customers will develop perceptions as to the "fair" price people should charge for a given type of product. If your products and services are perceived as similar to those of certain key competitors, the prices charged by those competitors will be used by potential customers as a benchmark for evaluating your prices. If you want to (or need to) charge more, it will be an uphill fight to differentiate yourself from those competitors and justify your higher fees.

Nonmonetary Aspects of Price

Some companies change the price perceptions of their markets by charging low prices, but making the customer do some of the functions normally performed by competitors.

An example here is Ikea. Although Ikea certainly charges prices significantly lower than most furniture stores, customers must carry heavy boxes home and assemble the furniture themselves.

INTERNAL CONSIDERATIONS IN SETTING PRICES

Although external factors should be paramount in setting pricing, internal factors cannot be ignored. The price you charge customers must at least exceed your costs to produce that product. This is called "profit."

Profit Calculations

You have to make profits. If you have funding, you may be able to sell at a loss in the early stages of product introduction, but you certainly cannot sell at a loss over the long term.

Conceptually, computing profits is easy. You add up your revenue and subtract your costs. Voila! Profits! (Or losses!) Except, like so much else in business, calculating profit is not so easy in the real world. Therefore, I consider these factors from a marketing perspective, not an accounting perspective. Accounting is governed by professional standards and by corporate and tax laws. And I want to be clear that I am not offering accounting advice. However, as long as you comply with the rules and keep proper books for the IRS, you also can look at things any other way you want.

Fixed and Variable Costs

There are two basic kinds of costs you incur when you run a business: fixed and variable. Fixed costs are what you incur just to open your doors. These include plant and equipment, payroll, and debt service. You have to pay these today whether or not you sell anything today.

Your variable costs are those costs related to producing each product. These can include raw materials, packaging, shipping, and postsale warranty support. You do not incur those costs if you do not sell anything.

It is clear to anyone who has run a business for more than 45 minutes that not all costs can be clearly lumped into one of these two categories. For example, your plant and workers may be capable of producing X thousand widgets per day. As long as sales are under that, you incur no additional costs beyond the usual variable costs. However, as sales increase beyond your basic capacity, you will have to start paying overtime, then adding additional shifts, and then acquiring more machines, and eventually having to add additional production facilities.

The critical thing to understand here is that your costs will always depend on your sales volume. In general, the more you sell, the lower your per unit costs will be, but not always. As in the above example, if you get close to your operational capacity, your costs related to producing additional products (or delivering additional services) may go up significantly. And, rather than incur those costs, it may be more profitable for you to raise prices, decreasing

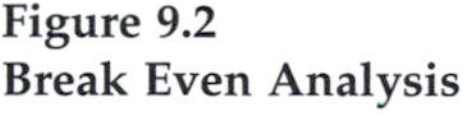

Figure 9.2
Break Even Analysis

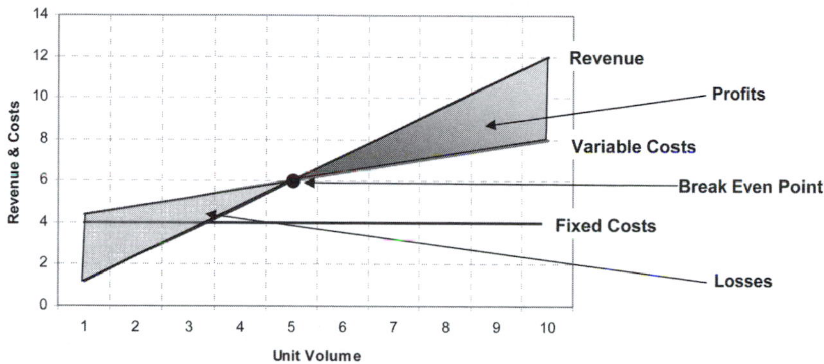

your unit volume (but, hopefully, not your revenue) back to where you can easily support it.

Break-Even Analysis

Marketers and managers use a technique called "break-even analysis" to establish the minimum sales volume necessary to cover costs, given a certain price. A break-even analysis plots the revenue gained at increasing levels of sales against the costs incurred to produce those sales.

Suppose your company makes widgets that are sold for $120 each and that cost $40 each to make, that is, the variable costs are $40 per unit. Suppose further that your fixed operating costs are $400,000 per year. The break-even analysis looks like Figure 9.2.

The break-even point would be where the gross profit (price less variable costs) from the sale of the products equals the fixed operating costs of the business. In this case, the gross profit is $80 per unit. It would, therefore, take a minimum of 5,000 units at a sales price of $120 each to cover the fixed costs, that is, break even.

Break-even analysis should not be used to set pricing. It should rather be used to assess whether the pricing you propose is going to work for you. Prices should always be set based on market, rather than cost concerns.

PRICING STRATEGIES

Maximizing Profits through Price Discrimination

People can vary greatly in the perceived value that they derive from various products and services. For some people, a particular product (e.g., a new air conditioner) may be seen as an immediate necessity (you are ill and are living in Phoenix in August), whereas others (e.g., residents of Toronto in December) would consider a new air conditioner far less important. As a result, different people are usually willing to pay different prices for exactly the same thing.

Merchants have known this for centuries. Even today, in many cultures, price negotiation about everything from appliances to taxi rides is the norm. In America today, we mostly negotiate over "big ticket" items such as houses and cars.

In most cases, we simply set a price for our products and accept whatever customers are willing to pay the price we set. This allows customers who would be willing to pay more to receive a "bargain," whereas customers who, by themselves, might still be profitable at a lower price will go somewhere else.

It is obvious, though, that we will maximize our profits if we can get each customer to pay the maximum that he or she is willing to pay. The problem is that we seldom know what that amount is, and we are usually unwilling to spend the time (which is valuable to us) to negotiate price with each customer. There are some strategies we can use, however, to reap some of the benefits of price discrimination.

COMMON STRATEGIES

Many firms consciously try to set prices based on customer characteristics related to their perceived willingness to pay. For example:

- Fashion-sensitive customers will pay more, so clothing stores charge higher prices when a new fashion is first introduced then reduce their prices later in the season. This same process applies to seasonal merchandise. We all know that December 26 is the best day to start stocking up on decorations, cards, and wrapping paper for next year.
- Price-sensitive customers will expend effort to get lower prices. Coupons and rebates require extra work. I also mentioned earlier Ikea's requiring that customers assemble the furniture themselves.
- Elderly customers eat earlier and are more price sensitive so many restaurants offer early-bird specials. "Senior citizen discounts" can also be found at entertainment facilities such as movies, museums, and theme parks.

Auctions

Auctions are one of the most effective ways of ensuring that buyers pay the maximum price they are willing to pay. Prospective customers continue to bid up the price until only the person who wants it the most remains. Ebay has become a huge success based on its ability to open the auction area to the entire world.

Product Line Pricing

One common practice is to provide potential customers with alternative versions of a product priced at different levels. Typically, there would be an "entry level," "no frills" version that would be priced low and a fancy, "high end" product line that would be priced much higher. Jos. A. Bank, for example, has men's suits priced from $295 to $1,295.

Some companies go so far as to have different brands for the products they offer at different price levels. Gap, Inc. has three different clothing stores: Banana Republic (at the higher priced end), The Gap, and Old Navy (at the lower priced end).

Price Adjustments

Many organizations try to take advantage of the differences in people's willingness to pay by first establishing a base or "list" price and then offering products at lower-than-list prices at certain times and under certain conditions. These adjustments may include:

- Markdowns in merchandise that is slow moving, obsolete, or uncompetitively priced.
- Coupons to encourage new users.
- Rebates on merchandise if the customer is willing to fill out and submit a form. Rebates give you the opportunity to advertise one price (list price less the rebate), while actually charging the marketplace a much higher price. This is because most rebates (estimates run from 80 percent to over 90 percent) are never redeemed.
- "Price bundling" means that you charge a lower price for product *X*, so that people will buy product *Y*. You may have noticed how many features you can get in a printer you can buy for less than $100. (At the time of this writing, Best Buy had thirty-one of them.) At the same time, the ink cartridges are very expensive and may actually cost more than the printer itself.
- Multiple-unit pricing or volume discounting is the common practice of lowering the per-unit price when quantities are purchased at once. This is the main pricing method for stores such as Costco and Sam's Club that essentially require you to buy in large amounts.

NEW PRODUCT PRICING

As an entrepreneur, you are more likely than most to be offering new products into the marketplace. Although a detailed discussion of how the marketplace adopts new products will have to wait until Chapter 11, two classic new-product pricing strategies are introduced here.

Skim Pricing

Skim pricing involves pricing your new product at a high level. You can use a skim-pricing strategy when you want to:

- Reap short term profits from pent up demand.
- Establish a high end market position.
- Take advantage of leading edge technical or intellectual property.

Skim pricing is best when:

- There is substantial pent-up demand.
- You want to establish and maintain a high-end market position.
- Your products and services are hard for competitors to duplicate.
- Your competitive advantage is short term and profits must be reaped immediately.

If you price high when your products are easy to duplicate, you are vulnerable to lower-priced competition. On the other hand, you may introduce a new product or service knowing that others will soon copy you. For a time you will be the major source for that product or service and recognize that you must get your reward while you can.

This is what the pharmaceutical companies do. They must invest millions of dollars to develop a new drug, and the testing and approval process can take up most of the time that they have patent protection. This means that the company may only have a few years to recoup that huge investment before generic drug manufacturers introduce much lower-priced equivalents.

Some companies use skim pricing as an introductory strategy, tapping the initial unmet demand and then lowering prices as initial demand is satisfied and competitors enter the marketplace. This was the strategy used by Apple when introducing the iPhone.

Skimming strategies can backfire, however. If the initial price is set too high, initial demand may be squelched before the product has a chance to take off. This happened to the original DeLorean automobile. Factory priced at $25,000 in 1981, there was such a demand that there was a six-month waiting list at many dealers. Quickly dealers began applying "additional dealer markups" of up to $10,000 to the orders already placed. According to some dealers I spoke with a the time, demand quickly dried up, leaving them with quick profits, but also some unsold inventory, slowing down or stopping the ordering of new cars.

Penetration Pricing

The alternative is penetration pricing. In a penetration pricing strategy, a company prices its new products relatively low (as compared to perceived value) to:

- Establish a customer base and get a foothold in the market
- Discourage competitive encroachment
- Build profit through economies of scale.

Works best when:

- There is long-term market potential that can be expected to be tapped over time.
- Potential competitors will jump in if there is a low price position they could take against you.

- Word-of-mouth "buzz" is expected to be important, so creating as large a customer base as possible as early as possible will greatly enhance the chances for success.
- Even early adopters need references before they buy.
- You are trying to establish a new product/service class or type.

The downside is that penetration pricing may promote the perception that the product has little value making it vulnerable to higher-quality, rather than lower-priced, competitors.

Ethical/Legal Issues in Retail Pricing

In the United States, there are federal and state laws that affect the pricing methods that companies use. In particular, these laws are concerned with the ways companies can and cannot discriminate among customers. If you are involved in different pricing for different types of customers, I recommend that you have a competent attorney review the pricing policies.

SUMMARY

- ☑ Pricing is how you get back the value you create with your products and services.
- ☑ Pricing should be based on the benefits people derive from your products and services, not what it costs you to produce them.
- ☑ Price elasticity determines how your sales volume will change when you change your price.
- ☑ Use break-even analysis to assess your pricing strategy.
- ☑ Skim pricing sets prices high to profit from pent-up demand.
- ☑ Penetration pricing sets prices low to build sales volume and market share.

10

Deciding on Your Marketing Strategy

At this point in the process, you have a good idea about:

- What you want
- What your marketplace wants
- What you are capable of
- Where you fit relative to your competitors
- What makes you special.

The question now is, what are you going to do about all of this?

WHAT CAN I CONTROL?

What you can do depends on what you can control. Let's start with what you cannot control. You cannot control:

- The marketplace
- Your competitors
- Your business partners
- The government.

You can certainly do things to influence them, but you cannot dictate their behavior. It would be foolish to base a marketing program on your ability to do so. What you can control are the aspects of your own marketing program. Marketers traditionally talk about "the 4 P's." I have added a fifth. These "P's" are:

- Product: What do I sell?
- Price: At what price?
- Place: Through what channels?
- Promotion: Letting the market know in what way?
  (and my fifth)
- Partners: Together with whom?

It is also important to remember that you probably do not have the resources to do everything you want. You are going to have to pick and choose.

MARKETING STRATEGIES

Your marketing strategy is your general approach to growing your business. There are only four fundamental ways to do this:

- You can sell more of your current products in your current marketplace.
- You can offer additional products to your current marketplace.
- You can offer your current products in a new marketplace.
- You can offer new products to a different marketplace.

These choices are summarized in what is called the "Intensive Strategy Matrix."

It looks like Figure 10.1.

Market Penetration Strategy

Marketing penetration is what most people think of when they think about marketing. It means continuing to do exactly what you are doing, but through advertising and other marketing methods, increasing revenue.

There are actually three very different ways you can do this.

Increase Sales to your Current Customers

This strategy involves increasing revenue from the same customer base. For example, if they are coming to your restaurant once per month, encourage them to come twice per month.

Figure 10.1
The Intensive Strategy Matrix

	Current Market	New Market
Current Products	Market Penetration	Market Development
New Products	Product Development	Diversification

One common way to do this is with frequent customer programs. Many years ago, the airlines started to offer special perks to people who would often fly on their airline. Free flights, upgrades to first class, free drinks, and membership in their airport club were among the benefits of using that airline.

Many retailers use similar strategies. Chico's, for example, offers everyday discounts to preferred customers as well as frequent special coupons in the mail and invitations to sales events exclusively for these frequent customers. Staples and Office Max send me coupons and gift cards on a regular basis. Charlie Brown's Steak House sends me $20 coupons every time I accumulate a certain amount of "points."

Many large corporations use this as their primary strategy. Top salespeople are assigned to single accounts with the goal of continuing to develop business with that one customer. Several of the large technology companies I have worked with have told me that as much as 70 percent of all new business growth comes from the same set of customers.

Even without implementing these kinds of programs, there is a great deal that an entrepreneur can do to encourage customers to buy more. Simple techniques include:

- Asking what else you could do for them
- Informing customers, through advertising, emails, or in-store information, about the complete range of products and services you offer
- Making the relationship more personal by developing a customer list (if you do not already have one) and sending emails or thank-you cards
- Simply remembering names.

For years, I patronized one particular salesman in the men's department at Nordstrom because he always remembered my name, the names of my family, my clothing sizes, and my general taste. I know a young man (younger than age 35) who makes over $200,000 per year selling Acuras. He claims he can remember the names and faces of everyone to whom he has ever sold a car, along with exactly what model they bought.

Attract Your Competitor's Customers

If your experience or analysis has shown you that you have some clear competitive advantage over your competitors or that one or more of your competitors have some significant vulnerability, you can exploit your advantage in your marketing program. This is what we did in the home heating oil program described earlier.

Convince Nonusers

A third alternative is to focus on people who currently do not patronize either you or your competitors. If you can convince them that your type of product or service would be of value to them, you can expand the marketplace itself. For example, Nabisco is marketing 100-calorie packages of some of their various cookies to people who are diet conscious and would, otherwise, be reluctant to eat cookies.

Convincing nonusers often involves offering an alternative value proposition that can appeal to people who may not have considered a particular product or service as an alternative to already understood needs. An example of this is The National Pork Board's "The Other White Meat" campaign.

Product Development Strategy

A product development strategy answers the question: "As long as I have all of these customers, what else can I provide for them?" In other words, how can I expand my product/service line to attract new customers?

I could easily cite dozens of examples of how companies do this:

- Applebee's Restaurant chain added a Weight Watchers section to their menu.
- Home Depot rents tools and delivery trucks.
- Hair salons provide manicures and pedicures, as well as selling hair care products.

Other common product development strategies involve "new and improved" products to replace current products and what are called "line extensions."

New and Improved

Anyone who has watched a daytime television show since about 1950 has heard advertisers claim that their product (soap, shampoo, toothpaste, etc.) was "new and improved." The idea here is to get potential buyers to redecide on their brand choice by letting them think that what they previously thought they knew about the advertisers brand is out-of-date. Of course, a great deal of support is needed to make those claims credible because "new and improved" has become a pretty stale phrase.

More powerfully, some companies make significant changes in their products to either:

1. Outdo the competition.
2. Make their current products obsolete so customers have to buy a new one.

We see examples of product improvements everywhere:

- Stores are constantly adding to their merchandise selection.
- Cellular phone companies are continuing to pack as many features as possible into as small a package as possible.
- Computer companies continually make their processors faster, their memory larger, their screens clearer, and their hard drives larger.

Some companies make the improvements in their products so large that their old products become obsolete. This can be an effective strategy if your product is durable and your market is saturated.

For example, every few years, Microsoft introduces new versions of its Windows operating systems and its Office productivity products. In each enhancement, dozens of new features and functions are added as well as many improvements to the user interface. Microsoft needs to do this because, eventually, almost everybody will be using their current operating system and sales will consist mostly of preloaded operating systems on new computers. But if Microsoft introduces a "new and improved" operating system (e.g., Vista) the new product buying cycle will start all over again. This will be particularly true if the old system is incompatible in some ways with the new system, driving everyone to catch up with the new standard.

Line Extensions

Line extensions are a product development strategy in which new products are added to an existing brand name. This can be a very powerful strategy and can also backfire. Many years ago, Tylenol was introduced as a pain killer that did not have the gastric distress problems often associated with aspirin. Today there are thirty-nine different versions of Tylenol, not counting differences in packaging. These line extensions are geared toward specific market segments (as discussed previously) and are designed to establish competitive advantage among those market niches.

On the other hand, if used too extensively, line extensions can erode the meaning of your brand. For example, at the time of this writing, Kellogg's has introduced three new products under their Special K brand: protein water, snack bars, and waffles. They seem to be betting that the Special K brand will mean "healthy" to potential customers. If it turns out to mean "healthy cereal," then these line extensions have the potential to confuse people into not knowing what Special K really means.

Market Development Strategy

A market development strategy evolves in answer to the question: "As long as I have all these great products, who else can I sell them to?" As with the other strategies, there are several ways to do them:

- Expand geographically: This is usually the first thing that comes to mind when thinking abut new markets. If you operate out of specific locations, open more. If you operate locally, expand regionally. If you operate regionally, go national. If you operate nationally, go global.
- Appeal to new market segments: Maybe one or more of your products has capabilities or benefits that would appeal to other market segments outside of your primary target market. As mentioned elsewhere in this book, restaurants sometimes appeal to older people by offering early-bird specials at reduced prices. McDonald's has an entirely separate advertising program focused specifically on children.

- Expand distribution channels: A third option is to sell your products in additional ways beyond what you do currently. A common tactic today is to open an online store. You may also place products with resellers if you currently sell direct; or sell direct if you currently sell through resellers. This is a technique many manufacturers use when they place "factory outlets" in outlet malls.

Diversification Strategies

Diversification strategies are about doing things differently. There are three types of diversification: concentric diversification, horizontal diversification, and conglomerate diversification.

Concentric Diversification

Concentric diversification looks a lot like product development. Companies using this strategy grow by expanding their product lines. However, in the case of concentric diversification, the products introduced are designed to appeal to new market segments, rather than to the current target market. Also, with concentric diversification, the products are technically related to the products the company already sells.

For example, Dell is trying to appeal to the home electronics buyer by introducing flat-screen TVs. In another example, I am currently working with a small software company that services cities and counties. It has determined that, with only slight modifications to its software, it could also begin to market to hospitals and nursing homes.

Concentric diversification works best when:

- The organization competes in a slow growth industry.
- The new product could enhance sales of current products.
- There are seasonal aspects of the organization's current products that could be balanced by the new products.
- The current product line is on the decline.

Horizontal Diversification

Horizontal diversification is the process of offering an entirely new set of products to your existing customer base. Here you are attempting to grow revenue by:

- Leveraging your customer base.
- Leveraging your market knowledge.
- Leveraging your brand name.
- Leveraging your distribution and sales methods.

Again, there are many examples here:

- Harley Davidson has been extremely successful with its clothing line.
- Almost every hospital has a cafeteria and a gift shop.

- Coca-Cola, Pepsi, and Budweiser sell all kinds of branded "gear."
- Cracker Barrel restaurant has a huge gift shop where people end up waiting for their tables.

Horizontal diversification works best when:

- Significant new revenues can result. It can take time and energy for management to learn a different kind of business. It needs to really be worth it.
- There is high competition and low margins. Your additional business can potentially bring in high profits because your fixed costs are already covered. For many office supply stores, their photocopy department accounts for less than 20 percent of revenue but up to 70 percent of store profits.
- Current facilities, infrastructure, and relationships can be leveraged.
- Current management has the skill and experience to manage the new efforts. This is critical. The new product class you are offering may have an entirely different set of operating parameters.
- New offerings increase current sales and customer satisfaction. In other words, you need to offer products that enhance, not detract from, your existing reputation.

Conglomerate Diversification

The last type of diversification is conglomerate diversification. Conglomerate diversification involves building revenue by going into an additional, entirely different business.

This is a difficult process. Despite the constant newspaper stories about companies acquiring other companies, acquisitions are quite hard to pull off successfully. The "remanagement" of one company often severely damages the informal social and operational relationships that made the companies successful in the first place, not to mention the additional, nonproductive, debt load that the combined firms often assume. For the entrepreneur, you have enough on your plate to make your own business a success. It is usually not a good idea to go into someone else's business.

There are some circumstances, however, where conglomerate diversification is appropriate. In particular, conglomerate diversification works best when:

- Organization is in a declining or highly variable market or industry.
- Capital, facilities, and managerial talent are available and can be utilized without putting core business at risk.
- Businesses can be acquired at appropriate cost.
- There is financial synergy with the acquired firm.
- Other circumstances demand that business risks be hedged.

Strategic Options for Ted's Fish Market

Given our analysis so far, Mike has any number of strategic options to grow Ted's Fish Market. These include market penetration, product

development, market development and diversification. Mike identified the following options for each:

- Market penetration
  - More aggressive promotional efforts in the local market area.
  - Hire a salesperson to develop commercial business.
- Product development
  - Mike's special spice mixes
  - Fish-related souvenirs to tourists
  - Packing and shipping
  - Seafood cooking lessons
- Market development
  - New locations
  - Tourists
  - Gourmets
- Diversification
  - No strategy yet, but perhaps in the future.

NEW PRODUCT ISSUES

Because you, the reader, are most likely an entrepreneur, it is also likely that new products play a key role in your business. For that reason, I want to discuss some specific issues related to marketing new products.

Pent-Up Demand and the S-Curve

New products should be introduced to take advantage of unserved or underserved market demand. As we discussed in the chapter on positioning, new products are most successful when they can be used to establish a new product class in the mind of the potential customer.

It is important to understand at the start that pent-up demand is just that, pent up. Some people are experiencing a need that cannot be satisfied by existing products or services. They might not even know that they have that need until, suddenly, a product (like a cellular phone several years ago) becomes available and they realize what they can do with it. However, once fulfilled, that pent-up demand no longer exists, and you are left with the residual product demand resulting from general market growth and the purchase of replacements.

The revenue growth curve for a typical new product might look like the S-curve in Figure 10.2.

There are three phases to revenue growth.

1. In the introductory phase, sales grow slowly as the product starts to become known in the marketplace. Initial customers consist mostly of

Figure 10.2
Revenue Growth S-Curve for a New Product

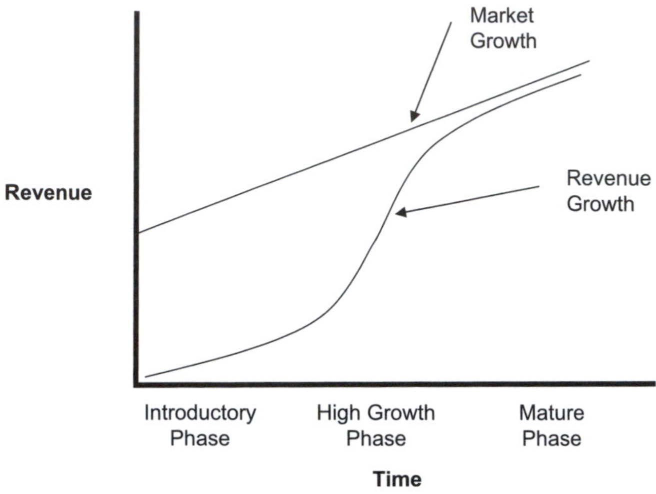

the relatively small proportion of Innovators (See Categories of Adopters, below).

2. In the high-growth phase, the untapped, pent up demand takes over. People who have needed or desired this product or service begin to flock to it. Growth takes off.
3. In the mature phase, what was formerly the pent-up demand has been tapped, and growth continues only at the rate that the market itself grows. Also, competitors are likely to have seen the rapid growth in the new product category and introduced their own competitive products. What is left is the general growth in market demand caused by an increase in the overall size of the market.

The big danger here for the entrepreneur is in not understanding that the growth experienced by almost any successful new product will be temporary. The temptation to believe that the high-growth phase will continue on is great. Many companies have overbuilt manufacturing capacity, overspent on overhead, and overcompensated executives and staff only to find out too soon that the rapid growth phase was coming to an end and that they did not have the next new product to take over.

The New Products Adoption Process

There are six steps in the process by which people and organizations adopt new products. It is critical to understand these when attempting to promote a new product because new product adopters will follow these steps in sequence. These six steps are

1. *Awareness:* They have to learn that the innovation exists.
2. *Interest*: They have to see how the new product might satisfy an existing or newly realized need.
3. *Evaluation:* They have to weigh the costs and benefits of new product against what they are currently using or doing.
4. *Trial*: They have to experience using product for the first time and decide whether or not the new product actually does what they expect it to.
5. *Adoption:* At this point, they actually buy the product.
6. *Confirmation:* Finally, over some period of time, they weigh expected versus actual benefits and costs and develop the habit of doing things differently with the new product.

Factors Affecting Adoption

There are several key factors that influence the likelihood that a new product will be accepted and the speed with which that acceptance will filter through the market.

1. *Relative advantage:* To what extent does the marketplace perceive the new product to have significant new benefits or other advantages over current ways of doing things?

   Cell phones have significant advantages over land lines, especially because the costs have become equivalent.
2. *Compatibility:* To what extent does the new product fit in with existing technologies? There are some products that do offer significant advantages over existing products, but the cost in money and time to switch would be too high.

   For example, the standard QWERTY keyboard, used by almost all English (and other) speakers, has long been known to be very inefficient. In fact, many companies have tried to introduce keyboard layouts that have been demonstrated to produce much faster and more error-free typing. But because the QWERTY layout is known to all, the costs of retraining people to use a more efficient layout would be greater than the benefit derived.

   This compatibility factor is one of the reasons why companies such as Microsoft have worked so hard to establish industry standards based on their products. If everything else must compatible with what you have, people must continue to use your product.
3. *Complexity:* How easy is the new product to understand and use? If it is difficult to use the new product, or certain features of the new product, people will simply not use the features that are hard to use or, perhaps, not buy the product at all.

   For example, the difficulty of programming an old VCR to record a TV program automatically became a cultural joke. This made DVRs (digital video recorders) like TiVo much easier to sell.

   To this day, I use less than one third of the features on my cell phone, although my thirteen-year-old daughter (who seems to have been born cable ready) uses almost all of the features of her much more complex phone.

4. Trialability: How easy is it to test the product out before you buy it? For the reasons mentioned above, many people want to know what they are getting into before they commit to buying a new product.

   Many technology companies have become experts at providing people with the ability to try their product before they buy them. Many software companies will allow you to download trial versions of their product to test out before you buy. There are even sites (e.g., www.download.com) dedicated to trial versions of products from smaller software developers.

   Another good example is what the AT&T cellular phone stores are doing with the iPhone. In each store, there is a large model of the iPhone, with a TV monitor instead of the small screen. Potential buyers can try out the various features and test the ease of use of this phone before they spend their $400.
5. *Observability:* Many people, especially the later adopters, like to see a product in general use before they will change to it themselves.

Categories of Adopters

There are several categories of adopters that marketers talk about. These categories and their relative size are shown in Figure 10.3.

- Innovators: Innovators are usually the first people to buy a new product or service. There are two primary motivations that innovators might have:
  - They have some pressing need that the products or services currently available cannot fill. These people are innovators out of necessity.
  - For other innovators, it is the newness itself that is the attraction. They will buy the latest technology or the latest fashions because they are new and different and will have little regard for social or collegial acceptance.

Figure 10.3
Categories of Adopters

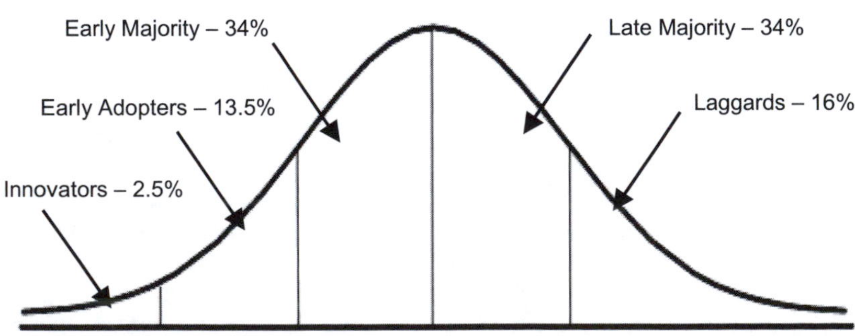

- It is important to recognize that these people are different, sometimes socially isolated, from the general population and that rapid acceptance of a new product by innovators does not necessarily mean acceptance by the general marketplace.
- Early adopters: Early adopters, like innovators, will try new products because they either have a pressing need for a solution to a problem or because they want to be seen as technically or fashionably cutting edge. However, unlike innovators, early adopters are more likely to be concerned with how they are perceived by others and are more likely to be recognized by others as expert and practical.
- Early majority: This large segment comprises that part of the greater marketplace that has an above-average willingness to try new products.
- Late majority: This is the part of the greater marketplace that has a less-than-average willingness to try new products.
- Laggards: This is the part of the marketplace that is resistant to new product innovations and will only adopt new products if they "have to." Even in 2008, I know a few people who do not have either computers or cell phones and have no plans for obtaining either.

PORTFOLIO ANALYSIS

There are a number of analytical tools that business people have developed to look at the various products and product lines that a business has in one glance. The most basic, and perhaps the most powerful of these, is the model developed originally by the Boston Consulting Group (BCG), one of the premier business consulting firms in the world.

Tool 10-A: The BCG Matrix

The BCG Matrix looks at the interrelationships among the various products, product groups, or business units within a company. Each product is categorized according to two dimensions, business strength and market growth rate. The following questions apply:

- Is the product a major or minor competitor in its marketplace?
- At what stage is the growth in market demand?

Whether the product is a major or minor competitor is not always easy to assess. It depends first on how you define the market. You do not have to be one of the major players nationally or regionally. If you are, for example, the number one purveyor of pizza in your local area, you are a major competitor. You can also use the business strength assessment you did in your Internal Factor Evaluation in Chapter 6.

In the second question, if the product has tapped into pent-up demand, then the growth in sales for the product will exceed the overall growth in overall size of the market. As the market becomes saturated (i.e., everyone who wants one now has one), growth in demand will decrease as discussed

Figure 10.4
The BCG Matrix

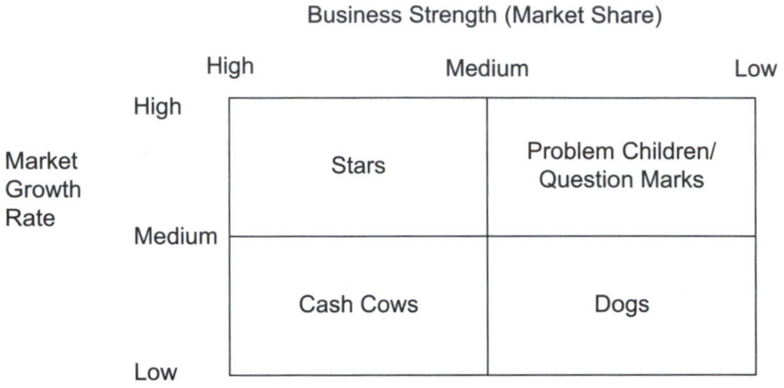

in the last section of this chapter. BCG considered the midpoint to be the overall growth in the potential market. Mature products are expected to experience sales growth below that of the total market due to competitive pressure.

The resultant BCG Matrix appears in Figure 10.4.

There are four cells in the BCG Matrix. The names of some of them you may have heard already. These four cells are cash cows, stars, dogs, or question marks:

- *Cash cows*: Cash cows are the company's solid, mature products and the main generators of a company's profits. These products have a strong competitive position in a market where the pent-up demand has been met. As long as this market persists, the company will be able to reap profits from these cash cows without significant additional marketing efforts. As such, they are extremely valuable resources to be nurtured and protected.
- *Question marks*: Question marks (sometimes called "problem children") are the new products that a company introduces into a market with pent up demand. The market is growing fast, but these products have yet to become dominant. Question marks can be considered a company's future. They are the future stars and, thus, the future cash cows.

  Question marks are usually a cash drain as the company continues to invest in marketing and product development to achieve product success. The goal is to build market share and become one of the dominant competitors in that market.
- *Stars*: Stars are the market leaders in high-growth industry. They build organizational visibility and credibility as the company seeks to solidify their long-term position in the marketplace and ensure that they become cash cows. As such, stars may continue to require ongoing investment and may not reach their peak profit potential until they actually become cash cows.

- *Dogs*: Dogs are nondominant products in low growth markets. The choice with dogs is whether to keep them or get rid of them (sell the product line or just close it). Companies, in general, should maintain a dog product if it either produces reliable, long-term profits with little attention or if it represents a core competency needed elsewhere in the firm.

Using the BCG Matrix

The underlying premise of the BCG Matrix is that:

- Organizations must generate cash from strong competitive positions in mature markets (stars and cash cows).
- To fund development efforts in new opportunities (question marks).
- Which will become tomorrow's stars and cash cows.

The flow looks like Figure 10.5:
The steps in using the BCG Matrix are as follows:

- *Step 1*: List all of the basic products, or product groups, that you offer.
- *Step 2*: Compute the gross profit (sales minus direct, variable costs) for each product or group of products.
- *Step 3*: Look at the rate of growth in sales for each product or product group.
- *Step 4*: Assess the competitive position of each product or product group.
- *Step 5*: Assign each product or product group to one of the four cells in the table.

Now, take a look at what you have and ask yourself at least the following:

- Do I have good products in the cash cow, star, and question mark categories?
- Do I have enough cash cows to support my business long term?

Figure 10.5
Product Evolution Cycle

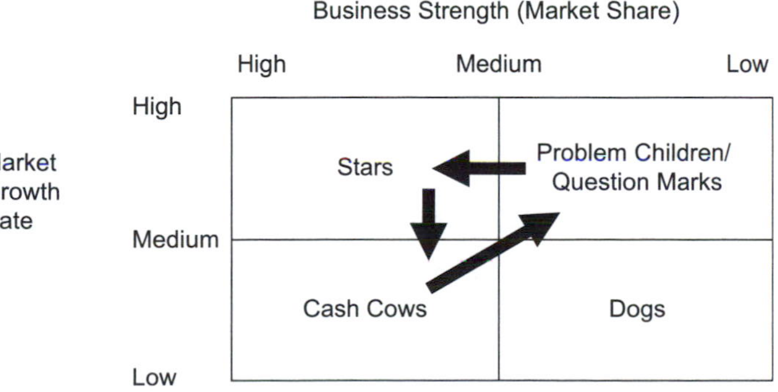

- If not, when can I reasonably expect my stars to become stable and profitable?
- Do I have enough new product initiatives to produce one or more solid stars?
- Do I have too many question marks (or stars) draining my profits so that I am too constrained in how I run my business?

Ted's Fish Market Example: Mike Jameson has the desirable problem of having many different strategic options. He will get into trouble if he tries to pursue too many of them, too fast. Although it is tempting to begin by starting with the products and services that are easiest to introduce, it makes more sense to introduce products that have the best chance of becoming long-term cash cows first. This is clear when we begin to think about implementation in terms of a growth strategy.

SUMMARY

☑ A market penetration strategy attempts to increase sales volume to your current market.
☑ A product development strategy increases revenue by introducing new products into your current market.
☑ A market development strategy increases revenue by opening new markets for your current products and services.
☑ Diversification strategies are used to reduce financial risks or take advantage of new opportunities.
☑ New products have a lifecycle.
☑ The rapid growth of successful new products usually comes to an end when pent-up demand is satisfied.
☑ Use the BCG Matrix to assess your product portfolio.

11

Developing and Delivering Your Message

The key to developing and delivering your message is to offer what people want in the way they want it offered.

I was once asked by one of my undergraduate students to help her boss who was buying the company he worked for. It was an automobile parts store, Parthenon Auto Parts, located in an out-of-the-way strip mall. The client, Don, had been the store manager for several years. The store owner was retiring and offered to sell the operation to Don at a fairly reasonable price, if he could secure financing.

I helped him prepare a financing plan for the bank, and all went well. He was now an entrepreneur and could finally realize his dream of building beyond the old, working-class neighborhood where the business was located. It was time to advertise.

The store sold foreign car parts. Don prided himself on having the largest stock of hard-to-find foreign car parts in a three-state area. His competitors were mostly the larger chain stores that stocked only those auto parts that had the greatest demand, relying on their customer's patience if they had to order a part they did not carry. But Don did not know how to capitalize on this competitive advantage.

We began, as usual, by talking to car parts buyers. In addition to the numerous repair shops in the region (the bread-and-butter customers of every parts store), there were also a large number of hobbyists who enjoyed working on their cars on weekends. One of the most common complaints we heard was that almost all independent parts stores closed around noon on Saturdays, making it very difficult for hobbyists to get what they needed without having to plan for it well in advance. (Anyone who has worked on foreign cars from the 1960s and 1970s knows that it is hard to plan anything in advance!) The first thing we recommended was that Don should expand his Saturday hours.

We then had to come up with an advertising theme that reflected the value that customers got from shopping there. He was not the least expensive nor was he the most convenient. What he did have was inventory and very knowledgeable salespeople behind the counter. (It is important to know whether the alternator for a 1967 Volkswagen can also work on a 1968 Volkswagen.) In other words, for hobbyists and other people who knew what they were doing, it "made sense" to shop at Parthenon.

We went with that theme and produced a radio commercial featuring a man named Charlie about to get up at 5 A.M. on a Saturday to go buy parts for his sports car. "Charlieeeeeeeeeeeee!" his wife (in the commercial) would say. "You don't have to drive all over town. It makes sense to shop at Parthenon Auto Parts. Now go back to sleep."

We elected to use a radio campaign for several reasons:

- It was affordable.
- By placing 15-second ads during afternoon drive time, we got to people while they were thinking about home, rather than work.
- We used the number one news station in the city for credibility because we had the best chance of reaching the more upscale people who had a higher chance of owning foreign cars.
- There was no need to show anything. The appeal was personal.
- The "Charlieeeeeeeeeeeee!" was spoken in a kind, but slightly impatient, voice and people remembered it. Sometimes customers even asked if "Charlie" had been in recently!

The campaign jump-started Don's growth. Within five years, he had expanded out to two more new locations that quadrupled his sales.

OFFERING WHAT PEOPLE WANT, THE WAY THEY WANT IT

Up to this point, we have been almost entirely thinking about what to do. We haven't actually done anything yet. However, at this point, we do know about:

- Our goals
- Our market
- Our competition
- Our products and services
- Our market position and value proposition
- Our pricing.

We know now that if we can effectively communicate our value to our market, we will be successful. We just need to know exactly what to say to get the impact we want. That is what this chapter is all about: developing and delivering the message.

INFLUENCING BUYERS

It is all about influence. It is all about influence because all relationships are about influence. That is what we do when we interact with people. We share our ideas, our goals, and our agendas with our friends and colleagues in the expectation that they will assist us. And we will assist them in turn. If there were no influence present, there would be no relationship nor any need for one. The same applies to business relationships.

Our only real choice regarding influence is: Do we create influence randomly or do we create influence consciously? In other words, do we simply act and hope something happens or do we plan our actions and maximize our chances for success? I think the latter is not only the only sensible choice: It is the only ethical choice if we are to assume responsibility for the results we create for ourselves and others.

THE BUYER DECISION MODEL

To influence any process, we must know how that process works. Influencing buyers is no different.

Figure 11.1 presents a model of buyer decision making that I have developed over my professional career.

The buyer decision model tracks the buyer's thought process from the first realizations of a need through the actual experience of the product or service purchased. The purpose of this model is to help you to identify the various key points at which the prospective customer may be influenced to purchase your product over that of your competition.

The idea here is leverage. If we can find that point in the decision-making process where the potential customer is most easily influenced toward our product, we can get a great deal more efficiency out of our marketing program.

Figure 11.1
The Buyer Decision Model

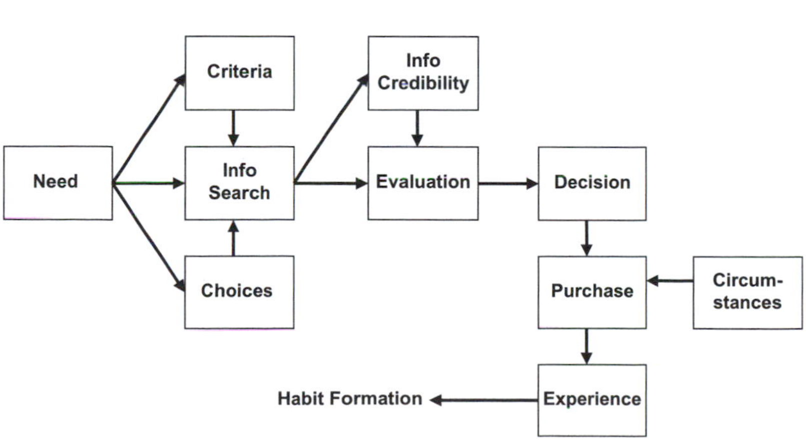

It is important to understand at this point that it is rare for consumers to proceed step-by-step through this process, although it is common for organizations to go through these steps in sequence. Consumers usually enter the decision process with much (sometimes all) of the process already completed.

That is why these influence points are so critical. In the Positioning discussion, I pointed out that it is difficult, if not impossible, to change someone's mind once it is made up. The trick is to find an area, idea, concept, or issue where the consumer does not have a preestablished idea and leverage that into an opportunity for that consumer to make a positive decision about you. The decision process is a powerful way to do so.

Need

Need is the motivation to seek out or respond positively to some product or service. The need could be physical (hunger, pain, or other physical discomfort), or simply a desire that some aspect of your life or your business be better. For example, your desire to improve your business motivated you to read this book.

Another way to look at need is as the answer to the question posed in Chapter 3: ''What do I want?'' To influence people at the need stage, we can simply remind people about the things and experiences that they may want. One example is Sprite's: ''Obey your thirst.''

Evaluative Criteria

If needs are the answers to the question, ''What do I want?'' then evaluative criteria are the answers to, ''How will I know I have it?'' Unless it is a completely new desire or circumstance, people generally have a notion of what it will take to fill their need. A simple need such as thirst may be satisfied with a glass of tap water. However, others may have a set of much more refined criteria for their thirst, for example, a French bottled water or a beer, or a Pepsi, or a glass of milk, and so on.

Evaluative criteria are clearest when we are buying an expensive item. Before buying an automobile or a house, we may spend a significant amount of time considering exactly what we want. For example, my wife and I spend most of our time working from home, so when we considered purchasing a home we knew that we both need offices. Then we ''needed'' a master bedroom, a room for our daughter, and a guest room. Then we wanted to have an informal family room addition to a more formal living room for entertaining. The list, of course goes on. We probably looked at thirty houses before we found one that fit.

There are two basic types of evaluative criteria: negotiable and non-negotiable. The non-negotiable criteria are the basic issues that define whether or not the need will be met. For example, when my family looks for a primary vehicle, it must have four doors. I have a relatively tall daughter, and she finds it very uncomfortable to get in and out of two-door cars. The car also has to have high safety and reliability standards Also, I do not care very much about color, but my wife and daughter do.

One of the most powerful things we could do to change people's buying patterns would be to convince them that there is an essential attribute that products like ours should have and that we are the only ones to have it. This is exactly what cell phone companies try to do when they introduce a new model to the marketplace.

Negotiable criteria are the features we will trade for a better price or those features that are nice to have but not essential. These are criteria that can potentially be used to set your products apart from the competition. Remember that I said at the start of this book that people do not actually buy products or services, they buy the experience that the product or service is expected to create for them. We can significantly influence buying behavior if we can convince potential consumers to look for a particular product or service attribute that only we have. For example, I do not "need" a GPS system in my car and have no problem driving a car without one. At the same time, I think it would be great fun to have one and, if the price is right, will probably get one on my next car.

The evaluative criteria step is one of the most effective influence points because people base their evaluative criteria on what they already know about the product class. If we can introduce new criteria into the decision-making process, we can potentially redefine the product class so that our product is uniquely positioned to meet the customers' needs.

Alternative Choices

If a potential customer is going to purchase from us, that customer first has to know we exist. The alternative choices step is where that potential customer identifies the alternative means he or she has for getting their needs met.

As we discussed in the chapter on competition, these alternatives do not necessarily mean alternative brands of similar products. Choices could be between product types or even different industries. For example, cable TV providers compete with satellite TV providers, each arguing the benefits of their specific delivery technology.

The primary method of influence here is awareness. The prospective customers must not only be aware that we exist, they must also know that we make up a viable means of having their needs met. We do not need to prove our case at this point, we just need enough of their attention to be able to do so.

Information Search

Once a potential consumer has experienced a need and identified alternative products or services that might meet that need, the consumer will look for information about those alternatives. The information sought will be about the extent to which each of these alternatives meets the evaluative criteria that the consumer has established.

The first place people look for information is inside themselves. In general, people will assume that what they "know" about various products is true. If they think that they do not already know enough, they will start looking for more information. People call this "shopping." We go to a store, look at the merchandise, ask salespeople, and try things out. There are many more places to look. People can look for and begin to notice advertisements in various media. They can go online. They can read articles and reviews in magazines. They can ask their friends. In fact many people find this part of the decision process to be enjoyable.

Information Credibility

Few people believe everything they are told. This is particularly the case in marketing where there is often the assumption that the advertiser is not telling the whole truth. As a result, people look for some means by which they can assess the credibility of the information they are receiving. The most credible information sources are those that:

- Are familiar with the product or service.
- Are independent of the company providing the product or service.
- Are credible in their own right.

That is why the best sources of credible information are usually friends who have used the product or service. Celebrity and customer endorsers try to fill the same role. Skillful salespeople try to assume the role of "trusted advisor" to their customers. (More about this in the next chapter.)

There are many other methods marketers can use to enhance the credibility of their messages. These include:

- Demonstrations
- Free samples
- Statistics and specifications
- "Independent" reviews
- Awards (e.g., J.D. Power)

Evaluation

The evaluation stage is where the potential customer puts it all together, assessing the pros and cons of the various alternatives he or she is still considering.

Decision

There comes a point where the potential customer will make up his or her mind, deciding which product or service to purchase. It is at this point that the customer becomes proactive, intending to make the purchase. If the customer has decided on our product, all we need do at this point is get out of the way. If the customer has decided on a competitor's product or service, there is usually little we can do at this point. Influencing at the decision point is difficult using advertising. However, it is one of the primary tasks of the salesperson and is referred to as "closing."

Circumstances

Once the potential customer has made the decision to purchase our product or service, we need to make sure that it is as easy to do so as possible. I'm sure you have been in the situation of wanting to buy something and being frustrated in that attempt because:

- The store was closed.
- The salesperson assigned to the territory was unavailable and no one else was allowed to talk to you.
- The product was out of stock or discontinued.
- The price had gone up.
- The people you tried to deal with were rude, ignorant, or difficult.

In these circumstances, all of the investment that company had made in marketing went right out the window. Not only were the customers stymied in their attempts to buy the product, they now had a negative experience that would deter them from buying anything else from that company or store.

On the other hand, customers also appreciate it greatly when they are treated in extraordinary ways. My wife and I bought an Acura several years ago from a dealer that prided itself on every aspect of service. It felt like getting a car at a fancy restaurant. If we buy another Acura, I would certainly buy it from that dealer, even though we now live three hours away in a different state.

Purchase

The purchase stage is simply the point at which the potential customer buys the product or service and turns into a real customer.

Experience

Marketers often think that they are done once the purchase is made. Nothing could be further from the truth. As I have said many times, people do not buy products or services, they buy experiences. Unless and until the customer receives the experience they expected, the real transaction is not complete.

It is critical, therefore, that marketing strategies ensure that people not only get what they expected, but also they know they are getting what they expected. In other words, information, technical support, warranty support, and so on should be as forthcoming after the sale as sales information was prior to the sale.

Your customer's initial postsale experiences are going to go a long way in defining the long-term nature of your relationship with them. These experiences will certainly determine what those customers say to others about you.

Habit Formation

In the discussion on positioning, we stated that people do not like to be wrong and that once their mind is made up, it is very difficult to get them to change. Those statements were made in the context of trying to influence someone to buy your particular product or service. Once the sale has been made and the customer is happy, that same process works in your favor.

In other words, if you can keep a customer happy, right from the start, that customer is very likely to remain a customer. This is often called "customer loyalty." We have to be careful here. Many, if not most, of your customers may be loyal not because they love you but because they are in the habit of buying from you and there is no compelling reason for them to change. Make sure you do not give them one.

DEVELOPING YOUR MESSAGE

Now that we have developed a good initial understanding of the processes by which people make decisions about acquiring a product, we can begin to consider how we will go about formulating a message that will influence them to buy our product or service.

But before we can formulate the specifics of that message, we must first understand the process by which people communicate with each other.

Understanding the Communication Process

A clear understanding of the communication process will not only help you to formulate your message, it will also help you to:

- Determine the most appropriate media for communicating that message.
- Identify the potential road blocks someone might experience in grasping that message.
- Overcome those roadblocks.

The model for the communication process that I use with clients and students is shown in Figure 11.2.

This model reflects both sides of the communication process: the sender's side and the receiver's side. For each component of the formulation and transmission of a message, there is a corresponding component for the reception and acceptance of that message.

Like the buyer decision model, these steps are seldom taken in sequence. When we communicate in daily life, all these steps seem to melt together. However, for us to develop a deeper, more powerful understanding of this process, it is necessary to break it down into its components and address each in turn.

Figure 11.2
The Communication Model

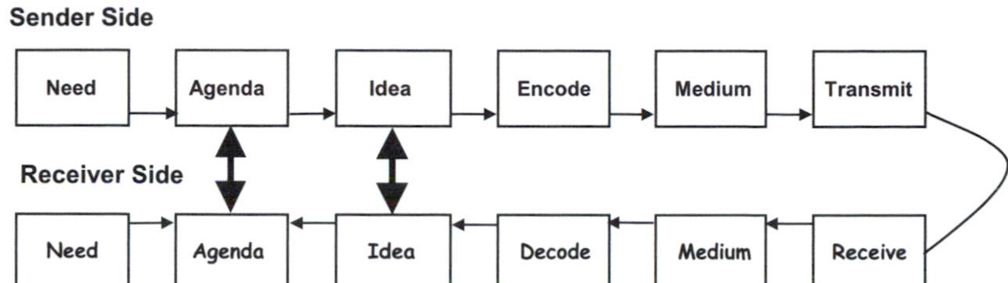

Sender Side

Need

Need on the sender side is just like need in the buyer decision model. It is the motivation to act. In this case it is the motivation that stimulates people to identify someone they think can help them satisfy that need and attempt to communicate with that person. In other words, this step reflects the first two steps of the relationship model discussed in the beginning of this book. What do I want? Who can give it to me?

Agenda

The reason we identify someone with whom to communicate is that there is something we want from them. That thing we want, be it behavior or just understanding, is our agenda for them. In marketing, that agenda is most often that we want them to buy our products and services. But this does not always have to be so. There are other valuable agendas that we may have when communicating. For example, we may want that person to:

- Remain happy with being our customer.
- Simply be aware that we exist, in case they ever need us.
- Recommend us to others.
- Partner with us in producing or promoting our products and services.
- Support our positions on legal or administrative matters such as regulations and zoning.
- Consider becoming our employee.

Idea

The idea is what we are trying to communicate. It is the thought that we believe, if understood by the other person, will influence them to do or think what we want them to do or think. Most of the ideas we try to communicate to others are simple and, to our eyes, clear. "Please take out the garbage." "I'll meet you at the restaurant at 6:30." "I love you." Yet any of us who have ever been in any kind of relationship with another human being know that there is always the possibility of confusion or "a failure to communicate."

In marketing, the idea we want to communicate is called the "creative platform." Once we determine what our creative platform is, we need to focus all of our efforts on getting this message to the right people, in the right way, and at the right time. Creative platforms are discussed more extensively below.

Encode

Encoding is the process of turning our idea into words, pictures, sounds, gestures, and all of the other specifics of formulating a specific message. It is at this point we pick a catchphrase or slogan and all of the other specific marketing messages we want to send.

Medium

The medium is the method we use to communicate. We all know about advertising media: TV, radio, magazines, newspapers, billboards, and so on. These are discussed in more detail in the next chapter.

For marketers, the keys to media selection are:

- The ability of the medium to clearly transmit our message, and
- The accuracy and efficiency with which that medium can reach our target market.

The media we use also affects how we encode our messages. For example, you can't have pictures in a radio ad, and there is only so much you can say or show in a ten-second TV spot. Therefore, we must consider the encoding and media steps at the same time.

Encoding has primacy to the extent that we need to get our key message across as clearly as we can. It may well be more important to sacrifice the efficiency or accuracy of the medium to get a clearer transmission of our message. Media has primacy to the extent that a clear message reaching the wrong target market is worthless.

Transmit

This is the step where the message is actually sent. Here the primary concern is timing.

Receiver Side and the Four Selective Processes

Receive

If the targeted person does not receive the message, it is wasted. People will actively seek out information about things that interest them or with which they agree and will actively avoid information that does not interest them or with which they do not agree. This process is called ''selective exposure.'' We select the messages to which we are willing to become exposed.

If we are to reach our target market with our message, we need to use media that are related to the interests of that target market. In other words, if you are selling golf equipment, don't put your ad in a sailing magazine (usually).

Medium

Just because the audience is exposed to your message, does not mean that they noticed it. Can you remember an interesting TV show you watched recently? How many of the commercials on that show do you remember?

Humans have an amazing capacity to pay attention to any of the hundreds of sensory inputs we are receiving at any time, or to tune them out. We have all had the experience of sitting through some boring event, speech, or lecture (but not in my class) and realizing that we have not heard a word that had been spoken in the last few minutes. This phenomenon is called ''selective perception'' (or sometimes ''selective attention'').

Therefore, if we want to communicate effectively, we must do something to first get the other person's attention. This is certainly true of marketing because people are experts in ''tuning out'' ads.

At the same time, what we do to get attention should not distract from our message. Sometimes advertisers use such a strong attention-getting device that people remember the ad, but not the product.

Decode

People will see and hear what they expect to see and hear. In other words, they will decode messages in ways that correspond to their expectations and beliefs. This is called ''selective comprehension.'' For example, if you agree with a politician, you will hear inspiration and leadership. If you disagree with that same politician, you will hear ambition and a pack of pandering lies.

It is therefore important for marketers to understand their target market deeply to understand how various messages will be understood and interpreted. We must communicate in a way that is congruent with our market's fundamental beliefs, otherwise we will not be heard.

Idea

Once we get through the first three hurdles of selective attention, selective perception, and selective comprehension, we will hopefully have successfully communicated the idea that we had in mind. In other words, successful communication occurs when the idea that we initially formulated is the same as the idea that the receiver thinks we formulated.

The question at this point is whether or not receivers think that the idea is persuasive enough for them to alter their behavior or thinking. To reach the point where your message is considered, the receiver must remember it. People tend to remember things that are either shocking (Where were you when your first heard that Challenger had crashed?) or relevant (What make and model was your first car?) This process is called "selective retention."

Agenda and Need

Finally, receivers of your message will compare the idea they think you communicated with their own agendas that are, of course, based on their own needs. If their resultant agenda for you is congruent with your agenda for them, great! We now have the potential for a relationship. Otherwise, no matter how effectively you have communicated, nothing happens.

SUMMARY

- ☑ Marketing is about influencing potential buyers.
- ☑ Use the buyer decision model to gain insight about where your best leverage points are for influencing buyers.
- ☑ Use the communication model to help you develop your specific message.

12

Getting Your Message out There

"Promotion" is the term that marketers use to refer to those actions designed to get their message out to the marketplace. There are four basic types of promotion:

- Advertising
- Sales promotion
- Public relations
- Sales

Advertising is paying to place your message in certain media: for example, on a television show or in a newspaper.

Sales promotion consists of the various special activities companies do to stimulate short-term sales. These might consist of contests, give-a-ways, "grand openings," free samples, or frequent customer programs.

Public relations is the process of developing a positive reputation. The objective is to encourage people to think well of you. This positive reputation, in turn, will facilitate sales.

Finally, sales is the direct process where one individual, the salesperson, interacts directly with another person, the customer, in an attempt to create a sale. The entire next chapter is devoted to this process.

Note: The promotional choices that you will need to make depend entirely on your own situation. There is no way for me to make any recommendations to you without knowing that situation. The best I can do at this point is to provide an overview of your options.

DEVELOPING A PROMOTION STRATEGY

Promotion is all about getting your message across to your marketplace. So a good place to start would be developing that message.

At the end of the last chapter, we discussed the communication model that describes the process by which messages are developed and interpreted. When developing a promotion strategy in that context, there are three main issues:

- The messaging strategy: What do I want to say? (The idea)
- The creative platform: How will I say it? (Encoding)
- Media strategy: Where, when and how will I communicate? (Media)

Messaging Strategy

At this point in your process of developing a marketing program, you should have a pretty good idea of who your current and potential customers are and what they want. And, based on your own capabilities, you have developed your value proposition.

It is your value proposition that you need to communicate. If potential customers understand your value proposition, and if your value proposition is powerful, people will buy from you.

The Creative Platform

The "creative platform" is the term many marketers and advertisers give to the core message about a company and its products that they want get across to potential customers.

This is a very important idea and requires some careful consideration. We already know that people are inundated with marketing messages from every quarter, every day. And we know that our challenge is cutting through that clutter with a simple, clear, and compelling message that will influence potential buyers toward our products and services.

Successful examples of creative platforms include:

- "The ultimate driving machine" (BMW)
- "I'm lovin' it" (McDonalds)
- "You can do it. We can help." (Home Depot)
- "You're in good hands." (Allstate Insurance)

Unfortunately, too many entrepreneurs and even professional marketers try to solve this problem by being clever. They develop a cute slogan that they think people will remember and dump that message out into the marketplace through whatever advertising media they can afford. Your message is way too important to be formulated in this manner.

I suggest that your try to come up with some yourself. Then ask your employees, customers, friends, and family to make suggestions. Then, before you implement one, try it out on some of your customers and get some feedback.

Media Strategy

Media strategy consists of three components:

- The selection of advertising media
- The extent of use of those media
- The timing of that use.

The rest of this chapter is concerned with these issues.

BUDGETING FOR PROMOTION

Advertising can be a "black hole" for your money. There is a vast array of choices and, in general, the more you do, the better your sales. But before you begin to develop your advertising program, you are well advised to develop a preliminary budget for that effort. This budget will provide initial guidance in your choice of media and frequency.

The most important idea regarding budgeting for your promotional efforts is that:

Marketing is an investment, not an expense

There are three common methods that companies use to determine their marketing budgets. These are commonly referred to as percentage of sales, competitive parity, and objective-task.

Percentage of Sales Method

In using the percentage of sales method, you decide what percentage of your gross sales you can appropriately assign to the marketing function and simply spend that. This method is simple, straightforward, and predictable. The only problem is that it is conceptually and operationally backwards.

The purpose of promotion is to generate sales. It is an investment in the future sales for your products and services. The percentage of sales method turns marketing into an expense—part of the variable cost of producing a product. In other words, with this method, the tail wags dog.

The results of using this method are that when sales are down, promotional expenses drop. This is exactly the time when you want to increase your investment!

Competitive Parity Method

The competitive parity method is just as bad. The intention of this method is to match or exceed your competitors' promotional expenses. In other words, with the competitive parity method, the other dog's tail wags your dog. You end up increasing your expenditures in response to competition, not ahead of it. You will never be better than second.

Objective-Task Method

The only sensible approach to budgeting for promotional investments is to think of promotion as an investment, just like plant and equipment or new product development. In other words, establish clear goals for your particular promotional program, estimate the financial benefit you will derive if those goals are met, then invest wisely as you would for any capital expenditure.

Now that you have some initial sense of what you must be able to invest in your promotional program, the following pages will make more sense to you. However, be sure to go back and revisit your budget, once you have a better sense of what your promotional options are.

HOW MUCH PROMOTION DO I NEED

Promotional activities involve an inherent trade-off among four principal factors:

- *Reach*: the number of different people who are exposed to your marketing message
- *Frequency*: the number of times, on average, that each person is exposed to the message
- *Richness*: the amount of information actually contained in the message
- *Cost*: the amount of money you are willing to invest in your program.

The more people you want to reach, the more it will cost. The more often you want to reach them, the more it will cost. The more information you want to impart to them, the more it will cost. The result is that you are going to have to make some hard choices regarding what you are, and are not, going to do in your marketing program.

Measuring Promotion Intensity

Promoters use several numerical measurements of intensity when comparing the costs of various alternatives: reach, frequency, gross rating points (GRP), or cost per message (CPM).

- *Reach*: This is the percentage of the target market that will be exposed to your message by that medium. Note that it should not be used as a measure of the percentage of people who will be exposed to your message. The important number is the percentage of people in your target market who will be reached. In promotion, there is always some level of "overexposure," meaning that people who would not be potential customers are still going to be exposed to the message, with little benefit to you. For example, if a particular advertising program reached 30 percent of the target market, its reach would be 30.
- *Frequency*: This is the average number of times someone in the target group will be exposed to your message.
- *GRP* (gross rating points): This is computed as reach multiplied by frequency and is a measure of the overall intensity of the message to your target market. For example, if the advertising program cited above reached that 30 percent of the target market an average of 4.5 times each, the GRP would be 135.
- *CPM* (Cost per 1,000 impressions): This is the cost to put your message out in front of people 1,000 times. In this measure, reaching 1,000 people once is the same as reaching 100 people ten times. It is still 1,000 impressions.

There is no absolute standard for what are or are not "good" numbers. In general, the higher the number, the more impact you are going to have. What these measures do is allow you to compare alternative media selection options to determine which gets you the biggest bang for your buck.

The Four Selective Processes

You can use the four selective processes to help you think this issue through: exposure, perception, comprehension, and retention. Remember that when you plan your promotional efforts well, these selective processes can actually work in your favor:

- *Selective exposure*: Selective exposure is best overcome by a careful placing of your promotional messages. The idea is to put your message where people would look for messages like yours.
- *Selective perception*: We have already established that it is critical to get people's attention. There are several ways to do this. You can command their attention by being loud or visually striking. Of course, you run the risk here of people remembering the attention getting device, but not the product or service.

  You can repeat the message over and over again (i.e., increase the frequency). Sometimes people are paying attention, sometimes they are not. If you repeat your message often enough, eventually you will reach someone when they are paying attention. The rule of thumb many promoters use is that a minimum of seven repetitions is necessary before you can be reasonably assured that people have noticed the message.

  You can also place your message where and when people would be receptive to your message. For example, if the ad for your restaurant is aired during a news show that is discussing war atrocities, you will probably be screened out, even if the viewers are exactly who you are looking for.
- *Selective comprehension*: In general, the simpler and clearer your message and its encoding, the easier it will be for people to understand. You can help accomplish this by using different ways to say or demonstrate the same idea, for example, show a picture of it in use and provide a description of its function.
  - Using different media with different capabilities.
  - Once again, repeating the message until it becomes clear.
- *Selective retention*: To get people to remember your message you can ensure that your message is relevant and timely. You can also provide a strong or shocking aspect to your message that will "anchor" it in people's mind. As mentioned above, you will run the risk that people will remember the shocking aspect, but not your name or product.

You can also repeat the ad to encourage retention. Here the process is slightly different that with selective perception. In selective perception, you want to concentrate your repetitions so that you maximize the probability that people will soon notice your message. In repeating for the purpose of overcoming selective retention, you want to space your repetitions out over time. This is called "spaced repetition" and is discussed further in the section on advertising.

ADVERTISING

When people mention marketing, most people immediately think of advertising. Advertising is that part of marketing where you (usually) pay someone to use their media to send your message. These media can include the commonly recognized advertising media of television, radio, newspapers, magazines, billboards, and public transportation. But, increasingly, clever (and not so clever) advertisers are reaching for unique media in which to place their ads. For example, there is an advertising agency that specializes in placing advertisements on commercial air flights. These opportunities include ads on overhead bins, beverage napkins, lavatory doors, and even the aircraft's wings!

By now, you should have a pretty good idea of exactly what you want to say and exactly to whom you want to say it to. You just have to select the right advertising media to use. Here are your choices:

Newspapers

In terms of total advertising billings, newspapers are still the largest advertising medium, accounting for nearly $50 billion in revenues annually in the United States. As of this writing, there are still over 1,500 daily newspapers and over 8,000 weekly newspapers published in the United States. Although there has been some decline in readership over the years, as more and more electronic media have flourished, that decline appears to have tapered off.

In recent years, newspapers have begun to use technology to improve their value as deliverers of news and as deliverers of advertising. Modern presses allow for the printing of multiple editions of the same basic newspaper with some stores and advertisements geared to specific geographical regions. Similar technology permits selectivity with preprinted advertising inserts.

Types of newspaper ads: There are three general types of newspaper ads:

1. *Display ads:* These are the printed advertisements found throughout any newspaper and represent the dominant form of newspaper advertising.
2. *Classified ads:* These are the smaller advertisements commonly restricted to specific pages.
3. *Supplements:* These are advertising flyers and other inserts created by advertisers, but distributed in newspapers. Many people buy the Sunday papers specifically for the advertising inserts.

The Advantages of Newspapers

Newspapers have several advantages that can make them an excellent advertising medium, especially if your target market is local. These advantages include:

- Targeting: Newspapers allow you to accurately target geographic areas either through the use of local newspapers or the use of regional editions of major metropolitan newspapers

- Flexibility: Newspaper ads can be placed in a wide array of sizes, in specific locations in the paper itself, and on specific dates.
- Currency: Ad placement deadlines are usually short, so newspapers ads can reflect current products and prices

The Disadvantages of Newspapers

Newspapers do have some disadvantages, however. These include:

- Quality: The reproductive quality of ads is generally poor compared to other print media like magazines, directories, and flyers.
- Short life span: People seldom keep newspapers (at least to read) longer than the current day.
- Clutter: There are lots of ads in newspapers and, because they are almost all in black and white, they all look alike.

Magazines

If newspapers are great for targeting geographically, magazines are excellent for targeting based on demographics and interests. The Standard Rate and Data Service (SRDS) currently lists over 3,000 consumer magazines and over 9,000 business magazines. A trip to the local newsstand or a major bookstore such as Borders will let you scratch the surface of the options available.

Magazines come in two basic types:

- Paid circulation, where the readers pay for the magazine, usually through subscription. Most consumer magazines have paid circulation.
- Controlled circulation, where the magazine is free for people who meet certain qualifications. There are a large number of business and professional magazines that fall into this category. My wife, who owns a software company, gets several free magazines geared toward IT executives.

Advantages of Magazines

Magazines have significant advantages, especially for companies that provide products or services to very specific audiences:

- Magazines are widely read. According to one estimate, 92 percent of Americans read some sort of magazine each month.
- Magazines are good for reaching specific target audiences.
- Audiences are particularly receptive when reading special interest magazines.
- Long life span. Many people keep magazines for months or, if of particular interest, years.
- Magazine formats allow creative variety. Ads can cover part of a page, all of a page, several pages, or even parts of several pages. Also many magazines have sections, usually near the back, where less expensive, classified type ads can be placed.

- The visual quality of magazines is far greater than that of newspapers.
- Sales promotion: Many magazines allow for the inclusion of coupons, samples, and information cards.

Disadvantages of Magazines

Magazines also have their disadvantages:

- Ads must usually be submitted well in advance of publication, sometimes more than three months, and, as an entrepreneur, you know that a lot can change in three months.
- Good magazine ads require professional assistance. If you are going to place ads in magazines, I strongly recommend that you get professional graphic help. Because the reproduction quality is so good, poor layout and production really shows.
- Magazine advertising can be expensive. For example, a single, full-page, four-color ad in *Reader's Digest*, reaching 8 million people, costs about $230,000, or about 3 cents per impression. On the other hand, you can put a full-page, four-color ad in *Home Business Magazine*, reaching 250,000 targeted people, for about $4,000, or about 1.5 cents per impression.
- Competition can make it hard for your ad to stand out. Although the per impression cost of *Home Business Magazine* may make it look like a good deal, remember that there will be dozens of other advertisers, including your competitors, with ads in that same issue.

Television

For many people, television advertising is the "fun stuff." It is the one media where you can provide motion pictures, sound, and even text. You can make them exciting; you can tell stories; you can make people laugh and cry.

At the same time, it is critical that you keep in mind that, from your perspective as an entrepreneur, TV is just another medium that may or may not be appropriate for what you want to do.

Advantages of Television

Some of the advantages of television as an advertising medium are:

- The ability to combine sound and moving images allows for:
  - Your products to be demonstrated.
  - Credible testimonials from users or celebrities.
  - A strong visual impact.
- TV can reach a large audience in a cost-efficient manner. Although TV ads can be very expensive, the CPM (cost per message) can be quite low.

Disadvantages of Television

Disadvantages of TV include:

- TV is expensive.
  - Commercials should always be done professionally and are costly to produce. Some of the major national advertisements can be far more expensive, per minute of time, than major feature films.
  - TV ads are costly to run. Air time for a 30-second ad can cost from $50 on a local cable TV channel late at night to more than $1,000,000+ for major television events such as the Super Bowl.
- There is lots of clutter. Earlier restrictions on number of commercials no longer exist, so there can be as much as nine minutes of advertising on a one-hour show.

Radio Advertising

Like local newspapers, radio is a great advertising medium for the locally focused entrepreneur. The SRDS lists over 10,000 radio stations across the United States. Some are located in major metropolitan areas, and many are located in smaller cities and rural areas. In addition, radio stations broadcast in a wide array of formats, including music of various genres, all news, talk, religious, and ethnic.

Advantages of Radio

In addition to its ability to target market segments, radio has the following advantages:

- Flexibility: Ads can be a short as ten seconds or as long as a minute. You can include voice and music. Advertising jingles got their start in radio advertising.
- Affordability: The prices for advertisements on radio are usually negotiated and can vary dramatically depending on frequency and time of day. If you are looking to reach large regional or national audiences, radio networks like CBS and Clear Channel can put together packages involving multiple stations in multiple genres. Although these large coverage programs can cost thousands of dollars per ad, small local radio stations can often provide 30-second advertisements for just a few dollars each.
- High level of acceptance: Many people, myself included, are "loyal" to one or two specific radio stations.

Disadvantages of Radio

Of course, radio has disadvantages, too. These include:

- Listener inattentiveness: Most people do not just sit and listen to the radio. They listen to the radio while doing other things like driving and working. As a result, it is difficult to get people's attention.

- Lack of visuals: Radio is only sound. You cannot ''show'' the product.
- Radio only happens now: Unlike newspapers and magazines where people can take as long as they want to review your ad, in radio (and TV) the ad is n for a specific time and then it is gone.

Outdoor and Transit Advertising

Outdoor and transit advertising includes billboards, signs, busses, subways, and a wide variety of other media that are limited only by advertisers' imaginations. However, because the time that people have to view these ads is usually so short (e.g., while they are driving), it is difficult to say much other than to provide some sort of striking visual. As a result, outdoor advertisements are most often used as either:

- A reminder (e.g., the food and gas signs along highways).
- A source of immediate information (e.g., ''One more mile to Fred's Diner'').
- A stimulator of curiosity (e.g., many Nike billboards).

Advantages of outdoor media include relatively low expense and the large number of per-person exposures if the ad remains in place for a significant period of time.

The biggest disadvantages include very short attention times and the fact that many localities ban or severely restrict them. The one exception to this local government resistance is transit ads, which tend to be encouraged because governments get direct benefits.

Directories

Directories list the names of people or companies, along with their addresses and phone numbers and, very often, display ads for the companies listed in the directory. Approximately 7,500 directories are published in the United States each year.

Directories can be of major benefit to entrepreneurs especially if you:

- Provide products and services to a clearly identified market
- Have a specific regional or local focus
- Provide products or services that do not change a great deal over time.

Directories are published by a wide array of organizations, for profit and not-for-profit. The most well known directory is the Yellow Pages, but directories are also published by:

- Chambers of Commerce
- Trade associations

- Economic development and tourist organizations
- Private firms

Strengths of Directories

- Directories are a shopping medium. Unlike most other advertising media, people look to directories specifically for shopping information.
- Most directory listings tend to be inexpensive and provide excellent return on investment.
- Directories offer flexibility and have a long life, usually at least one year.

Weaknesses of Directories

Directories have an extreme level of clutter, especially in the Yellow Pages, where all the ads seem to look alike. Some Yellow Pages directories are improving this situation somewhat by adding additional colors like white, red, and blue.

Ads cannot be changed for months. If something major changes in your business (e.g., a move to a new location), you are still stuck with your directory ad.

Internet Media

The Internet is the fastest growing advertising medium. Ad revenues for this medium were around $12 billion in 2006 and are expected to continue to grow at about 20 percent per year into the foreseeable future.

Your Home Page

In today's business world, the most powerful advertising you can do is to have an excellent World Wide Web Home Page. One of the first things people do, especially for any kind of professional products or services, is to check out your home page to get a fuller sense of who you are and what you do.

Of course you should start by obtaining a memorable URL or Web address. You might even want to obtain Web addresses similar to your own so that competitors don't grab them. For example, if Mike Jameson gets www.tedsfishmarket.com, he might also want to get tedsfishmarket.net and tedsfishmarket.us.

There are as many types of home pages as there are businesses, and whatever rules I might want to propose here could easily be wrong for your business. I will suggest strongly, however, that you forgo any temptation to make your Web site all about you. Make your Web site a place of as much value as you can for your customers. For a more detailed explanation of how to get a Web page and further utilize the Internet and the World Wide Web in your business, I recommend *Entrepreneur's Guide to Managing Information Technology* by C.J. Rhoads published by Praeger in 2008.

SALES PROMOTIONS

Sales promotions are special actions, beyond advertising, that are designed to create short-term motivation to buy. Common sales promotion techniques include:

- Sales
- Coupons
- Contests
- Special events
- Bonus gifts
- Free samples
- Frequent customer programs

A thorough discussion of when and where to use these various techniques would require a book of its own. However, I would like to share a few ideas:

- Sales promotions should always support your core value proposition and be consistent with your advertising and other promotional activities.
- Consistently using price promotions as a means of stimulating sales just trains your customers to wait until the sale before they buy.
- Any gifts, promotional giveaways (e.g., pens, calendars, etc.) should not only support your core value proposition, but should also be of a quality consistent with what you are claiming in your industry. I have seen many companies impeach their own quality claims by giving away cheap stuff to actual and potential customers.
- Free items have their greatest impact when the customer is not expecting them. In New Orleans, they use the word "lagniappe" to refer to any small gift or extras given to the customer at the time of purchase. It could be as large as a gift card to a nice restaurant to a couple who purchased a house of car from you to a balloon for a small child in a restaurant or store. The cost can be very low, but the impact will be high.
- You will get better leverage from you sales promotions if you can make them fun, without trivializing your brand or if you tie your promotions into some "worthy" not-for-profit program.

PUBLIC RELATIONS

Public relations (PR) is the process of developing a positive reputation in your market and community. Here, the object is not so much to motivate people to buy from you as it is to encourage people to think well of you. There are two primary ways entrepreneurs can accomplish this: media stories and sponsorships.

Media Stories

Getting someone to say something nice about you is always more powerful and more credible than saying something nice about yourself. And news media still have great credibility, especially in local markets. Getting your name or the name of your business in the newspaper is a positive way creates long-term good feelings about you and what you do.

Here are just a few hints:

- It is not enough to be seen to do good. There must be solid truth behind what you want people to say about you. In today's overcommunicated society, it is very hard to hide negative facts for long as many politicians, celebrities, and business people have found out.
- Do the right things for your customers and community and the word will eventually get out. Be patient.
- Make contacts with people in the media or with people who know people in the media. Reporters, even local reporters, see piles of press releases or have people constantly coming to them with requests for stories. If they do not already have a positive impression of you or you have not been referred by someone known to them, you have little chance of getting their attention.
- If you are operating in a larger metropolitan environment or if you need to make something happen quickly, consider hiring a professional PR consultant. These people generally know how to get to the right reporters and how to frame a story so that it becomes newsworthy.

Sponsorships

Sponsorships can be one of the most powerful and cost-effective of advertising methods, especially for locally based firms. The opportunities here are many, including:

- School and intramural sports teams
- Local museums and other not-for-profit attractions
- Adopt-a-highway, antilittering programs
- Hospitals
- Community programs such as parades and other holiday events.

These sponsorships become even more meaningful if you, the entrepreneur, take the time to assist one or more local organizations as a volunteer or even a Board member.

Sponsorships allow you and your firm to be seen in a very positive light as not only product or service providers, but also as contributing members of the community at large.

SUMMARY

☑ Promotion is an investment, not an expense.
☑ Advertising plans must consider reach, frequency, richness, and cost.
☑ There is a vast array of choices for advertising media.
☑ Sales promotions are special activities to stimulate short term sales.
☑ Public relations help build awareness and reputation.
☑ Sponsorships are an excellent way for entrepreneurs to promote their businesses.

13

Selling Effectively and Ethically

The goal of an effective marketing strategy is to enable the sales process. Selling works most effectively when it is ethical and straightforward.

LEARNING TO WATCH AND LISTEN

I was once asked to help out a store that sold plants. This company was actually in the business of providing plants to offices in Washington, D.C. They had a warehouse out in the suburbs that they also opened to the public.

This was not your ordinary plant store. For one thing, it was huge. It was close to one quarter of an acre inside. Also, interspaced among the hundreds of plants were about two dozen parrots, macaws, and other tropical birds. It was like walking into a South American Jungle: heat, humidity, and the crying of birds.

This company had called because their retail sales were far less than they had hoped when they had opened. They had expected that the experience of visiting their facility would have drawn lots of people in to visit, and this would be reflected in their sales. It was not.

When I went to visit them, I brought along a friend of mine who was a very successful salesperson for a major technology company. I wanted to get as broad a perspective on the situation as I could. We had made arrangements with them to stay for about two hours and observe the salespeople in action.

For most of the first hour, I was talking with the salespeople, while my friend just sat and watched customers. I found the salespeople to be knowledgeable, friendly, and energetic. It was not clear to me yet why the company was having problems. As I was discussing this with my friend, at one point he stopped me and directed my attention to the front door.

What I saw was a woman coming into the store and stopping short just inside the door. She seemed to be surveying the huge room and listening to the birds. Immediately, one of the salespeople came up to her. "Can I help you," he said. "No, thank you," she replied, "I am just looking." My friend told me to keep watching. The same basic scene was repeated three more times in the next ten minutes.

What is happening, my friend pointed out, was that people were amazed at the place when they first came in. Rather than let people soak in how interesting the place was, the salespeople were breaking in immediately. The result was that the salespeople were succeeding in getting denied permission to speak to their customers in their own store! No wonder sales were too low.

After some discussion, we made two key recommendations:

1. Customers coming into the store should initially be left alone to enjoy being in that wonderful environment. Only when a customer had stopped for several seconds to examine a plant (not a bird) should a salesperson approach them.
2. The salespeople should not ask "Can I help you?" That is just an invitation to be rejected. We suggested that salespeople should be trained to ask one of the following two questions:

   - "Are you looking for something for the home or something for the office?"
   - "Are you looking for something for yourself or as a gift?"

The answers to these questions are almost always one of the alternatives offered, and that answer provides the salesperson the opportunity to probe more deeply into the customers interests.

A simple change to the sales method made a difference. My client accepted our recommendations and retail sales went up 50 percent almost immediately.

ASKING CLEARLY AND DIRECTLY FOR WHAT YOU WANT

For many people, giving people what they want is much easier than asking for something for themselves. Most of us have been taught from childhood not to be greedy or selfish. We have been taught to think poorly of people who are too unabashedly direct in going for what they want. One of the reasons salespeople have developed such a poor reputation is because they are often pushy and too direct.

In sales, trying to avoid this reputation is often manifested as "closing reluctance" or fear on the part of a salesperson to ask the customer for the order. In advertising, especially mass media advertising, the impersonal nature of the communication makes asking for the sale much easier and, as a result, is responsible for much of the negative attitudes people have about advertising.

In business as in anywhere else in life, if one does not ask for what one wants, he or she must rely on luck, fate, or mind reading on the other's part to get his or her needs met. In business, this reliance on chance can be fatal. Therefore, techniques and attitudes must be developed that encourage a businessperson or salesperson to ask for the sale and maximize the potential of a positive response from the customer for doing so.

The ideas presented so far in *The Entrepreneur's Guide to Marketing* make understanding this step much easier. The customer is there because he or she has a need and wants to buy some product or service (hopefully, yours) to satisfy that need.

Ultimately, customers will choose for themselves which product or service to buy, and they will do so for their own reasons. If the salesperson has been sincerely interested in helping the buyer choose, then the chance of a positive response is greatly increased, and a negative decision on the part of the customer will not be taken personally.

BUYER ROLES

There are several distinct roles that people can play in the buying process:

- Users: those people who will actually use the product or service or who will derive the greatest benefit
- Decision makers: those people who ultimately make the decision as to which product or service will be purchased
- Gatekeepers: those people who, sometimes at the direction of the decision maker, are responsible for gathering the information the decision maker needs
- Influencers: those people whose opinion is sought and valued by either decision makers or gatekeepers
- Signature authorities: those people who are authorized to commit the funds necessary to make the purchase.

Although discussions of buyer roles are usually reserved for higher end, business-to-business marketing, even in casual, retail situations, these roles may be very important. Anyone who has ever made a sales presentation to a husband and wife will know this.

When doing business-to-business sales presentations, understanding and appreciating these roles can be critical. This is particularly the case with gatekeepers. Gatekeepers are often administrative staff or junior professionals assigned the task of developing information about purchasing choices and making recommendations to the decision maker. Many companies mistakenly train their salespeople to try to bypass the gatekeepers to get to the decision makers. However, in today's business environment, most decision makers have neither the time nor the interest in seeing salespeople or gathering information themselves. They assigned that to the gatekeeper. Even if they do want to meet with certain vendors, it will be the gatekeeper that usually decides who the decision maker will see. In other words, take the role of the gatekeepers seriously and treat them with respect.

Figure 13.1
Stage 1 Decision Space

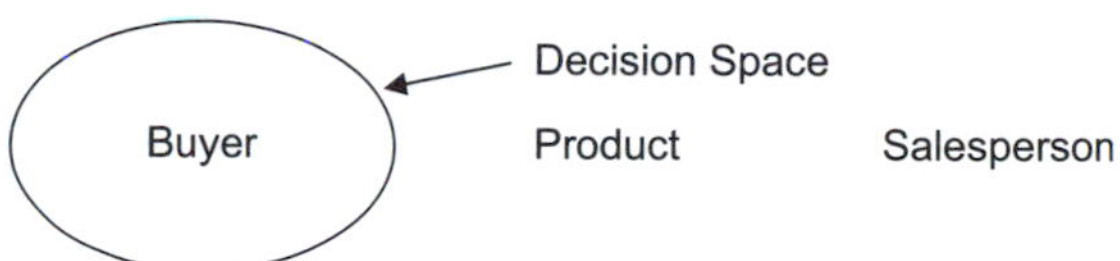

DECISION SPACE

The sales process can be more clearly understood through the concept of "decision space." Decision space is where the potential customer makes the decision on the product or service. The decision space encompasses the entire buyer decision model, including all of the choices and considerations that a potential customer includes in making the decision whether or not to buy a particular product or service.

Three Stages of the Decision Space

The sales process can be seen as the evolution of the decision space through three stages:

- *Stage 1*: Buyer alone: In the first stage, the buyer world is theirs alone. At this point the salesperson has no influence, and the salesperson's product may or may not be among the choices the buyer is considering. This situation is shown in Figure 13.1.
- *Stage 2*: Product inclusion: In Stage 2, the salesperson's product is included in the buyer's decision space. This is what most salespeople strive to do: ensure that the potential customer is considering the product and has all of the credible information that they need to make their decision. At this stage, the decision space has expanded as in Figure 13.2.
- *Stage 3*: Salesperson inclusion: In Stage 3, the decision space has expanded to include not only the salesperson's product, but also the salesperson, herself. In other words, the salesperson has become an integral part of the decision process: a "trusted advisor" to the buyer, assisting that buying in making the decision. This expansion is shown in Figure 13.3.

Figure 13.2
Stage 2 Decision Space

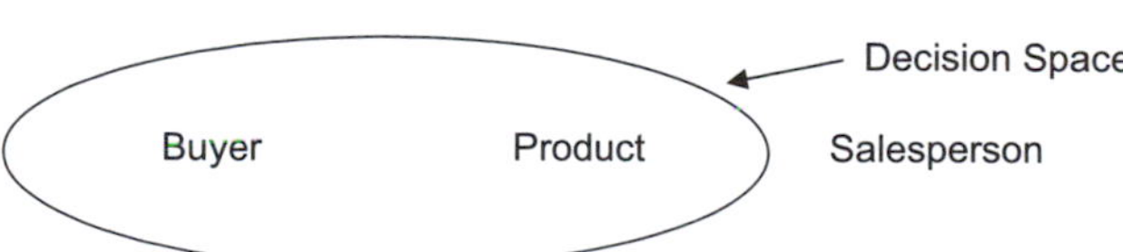

Figure 13.3
Stage 3 Decision Space

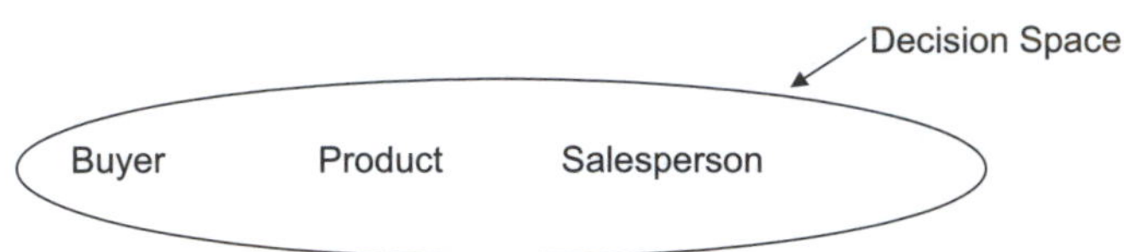

TRUSTED ADVISOR

Initially, the buyers have total control of the decision space, because it is made up entirely of them and their beliefs. It is the job of salespeople to convince the buyers to share that space and allow them to influence the decision. Better yet, salespeople would actually like to become the buyer's partner in making that decision. In other words, salespeople should endeavor to become the buyer's trusted advisor.

The key concept here is trust. This means that the salesperson must always act ethically and honestly. The customer must believe that:

- The salesperson is trying to help, not just make the sale.
- The information provided by the salesperson is complete and true.
- The salesperson is a reflection of the overall honesty of the whole organization.

As we go through this discussion of personal selling, keep the concept of "trusted advisor" in the back of your mind at all times. It is what drives everything else I have to say about sales.

THE SALES PROCESS

Despite that fact that there are literally thousands of books on selling and hundreds of different "models" of the sales process, eventually the sales process comes down to seven below:

1. *Prospecting*: finding potential buyers with whom to talk.
2. *Qualifying*: assessing whether they need the product and are able to buy it.
3. *Preapproach*: preparing for the presentation by learning as much as you can about the company or person and preparing your presentation specifically for them.
4. *Presenting*: providing relevant information to the buyer in response to his or her needs.
5. *Clarifying*: responding to whatever objections the potential buyer might have.
6. *Closing*: asking for the order.
7. *Delivery*: ensuring that the buyer receives what was agreed.

I discuss each of these in turn.

Step 1: Prospecting

You can't sell if there is no one to sell to. Prospecting is that part of the process where you find people who are willing to discuss your products and services with you. There are two basic ways to do this: go find them or have them find you. In most cases, you will end up doing some of both.

The Self-Identified Prospect

"Having them find you" is usually the best way to obtain prospects. If someone is coming to you inquiring about your product or service, at least you know that that person has some basic level of interest in what you are doing.

Creating this type of prospect usually involves a promotional program where you create awareness of your products and services and a means for interested people to contact you. Those TV ads that loudly proclaim "operators are standing by," along with a flashing, oft-repeated 800 number are obvious examples. On the other hand, all good advertising includes what is termed a "call to action." The call to action encourages the reader/viewer to "find out more," "visit our showroom," or "check us out on the Web at www.(nameofthebusiness).com."

Other promotional activities designed to create sales prospects include trade shows, telemarketing, yellow pages, and direct mail.

I have had good results using direct mail to generate prospects for technology and consulting companies I have worked with. I generally offer some sort of informative short book about the issues our product or service addresses and mail it to people who are likely to have an interest in that issue. Those who ask receive a free copy of the book, and the book becomes the initial basis of a conversation about the issue. We can then quickly find out if they are interested in our product, or just the book. I have had people who received a book but had no interest in the product call me several years later when they did have a need.

Another way to get people to come to you is to open a store. If you have a stand-alone store, you will, of course, have to do all of the same promotional work to make people aware of you and to get them to actually visit you. One of the reasons stores congregate in malls is because there is "traffic," that is, people who have come to the mall for some purpose other than visiting that particular store. Many of these mall visitors will pass that store, however, and some will stop in to look around.

Finding Prospects Yourself

This process, often referred to as "prospecting," can be either one of the most arduous or most enjoyable parts of the sales process. (I have experienced both.) Because prospecting is so essential to successful sales, I spend some significant space on it.

Here are some of the most common prospecting methods used by salespeople:

Loyal customers. Your absolute best source of prospects is your current, happy customers. No one is more credible to a potential customer than a real customer.

Salespeople should always ask their customers if they are aware of anyone else who might be interested in that product or service, and if the customer would mind if his or her name were used. Customers are usually happy to do so and may even make the initial phone call for you to pave the way. This can lead to a chain of referrals where one happy customer creates more who create more, and so on. This, in fact, is the basis of such referral based marketing programs as Amway and Longaberger Baskets.

Referrals should always be rewarded in some way, but usually not with cash. Some of the more effective ways that I have seen referrals rewarded include:

- *A thank-you note*: Whatever else you do, send a personal, handwritten thank-you note on nice stationary. In today's overcommunicated world, taking the time to actually write a note means a great deal. And it shows that you have "class."
- *Gifts*: I knew a real estate agent who provided a gift certificate good for a dinner for two at a very nice restaurant to any agent that sold one of his listings. Other gifts can include tickets to shows or sporting events, plaques, or department store gift certificates.

  Just be careful here. In government environments and most corporate environments, employees are not allowed to accept gifts from salespeople. In cases where employees can accept small gifts (e.g., less that $25), I sometimes recommend provide a subscription to an interesting periodical, for example, a travel magazine, a science magazine, or a professional journal. You can usually get ideas about their interests from their office. Every time they receive their copy of that periodical, they will be reminded of you.
- *Credit toward future purchases*: I knew an office supply firm that gave a $50 merchandise credit to anyone who referred a new account.
- *Free services*: I know a high-end software company that provides a free day or consulting or training to any client who refers a new customer.
- Others in your firm: If you work for a company with more than one person in it, the other people in the company are sure to know other people who know other people, and so on. Everyone in your company should be constantly on the lookout for potential customers.
- Rewards are also needed here, but again, care must be taken. Rewards to employees for referrals must be seen to be significant, especially if your salespeople are very well compensated from turning that lead into a sale. At the same time, you do not want the incentives to be so high that employees will be trying to do the salespeople's job instead of their own.
- *Networking*: Put simply, you have to be out there meeting people and telling your story. Networking is the key skill of this century. Many business scholars and analysts (notably Tom Peters) believe that it is our network of contacts, not our job, that will provide us professional security from now on.

To understand how networking works, I strongly recommend the book *The Tipping Point*, by Malcolm Gladwell (Little, Brown & Company, 2002). In this book, which spent 28 weeks on the *New York Times* bestseller list, Gladwell talks about three different types of key people in the networking process: connectors, mavens, and salesmen.

- Connectors: These are the people who seem to know "everyone." Connectors seem to collect people. They have a huge Rolodex/database of people, many of whom they keep in contact with on a regular basis.
- Mavens: These people are the experts on a particular subject, the people other people look to for knowledge and insight. Mavens are valuable because they lend credibility.
- Salesmen: Salespeople have the skill of persuasiveness. They are the ones who "sell" the ideas to other people, using the maven's credibility, introduced by the connectors.

Bird dogs: Bird dogs are people who are intentionally looking for leads for you. These can simply be people you know who are connectors and who have agreed to help you out for whatever reason.

There are also some people who do this professionally, taking a "finders fee" of anywhere from 1 percent to 10 percent of the amount of any sales made as a result of their leads. If you are trying to introduce a product into closely knit industry (e.g., the federal government), one of these representatives might be very valuable to help you get started. The good ones are often well known former members of that industry (such as lobbyists) and can quickly introduce you to the "right" people for a fee. Before you retain someone in this capacity, however, check their references carefully to make sure that they have a track record of delivering customers.

Professional associations: Professional associations are excellent ways to meet people who have an interest in what you do. They are also great ways to get to know others in your industry and keep abreast of industry trends and competitive activities. According to the *Encyclopedia of Associations*, there are over 23,000 trade associations in the United Stated and over 135,000 worldwide.

I suggest that you get involved with at least one professional association, preferably one that has local chapters. You will develop lasting friendships and gather information and insights you can get nowhere else.

In addition, you might consider getting involved with one or more associations serving your target market(s), if there are any. Keeping up-to-date with trends in those industries and developing a deeper understanding of industry concerns can be invaluable in marketing and new product development.

From a sales perspective, you will also get the opportunity to meet potential customers in a less formal environment. You can also use associations to continue to build your professional network and referral base.

Civic associations: If your products and services are geared more to consumers than corporate customers, you should consider joining local or regional civic associations. These could include your local Chamber of

Commerce, Rotary Club, Arts Council, or the Board of Directors of a local college or foundation. When I was a partner in an advertising agency, most of our clients came through these sources.

Also, it is just plain good to give back to your community whether or not you reap a direct benefit.

Trade shows and conferences: Trade shows and conferences are excellent ways to develop contacts and leads. If you are a member of an association, you will probably already be attending their annual or periodic conferences.

Trade shows are even bigger events. There is usually a "show floor" where vendors such as yourself can set up a booth to display your wares. This area can comprise just a few thousand square feet outside of a hotel ball room or hundreds of thousands of square feet in a major metropolitan convention center. Conference attendees will usually visit the trade show floor and peruse the various display booths. This is your chance to meet potential customers and discuss their particular needs. In many of these shows, visitors will be key decision makers.

Cold calls: Cold calls are many salespeople's least favorite method for generating sales leads. Cold calling involves either telephoning or dropping in on people who have not previously expressed any interest in your product or service and who are not expecting your call or visit.

Teaming with other firms: One more way of generating leads is by partnering with noncompetitive firms that are also serving your target market. Salespeople in those firms are calling on people who may be potential customers for your products or services, as well as those that salesperson represents. Sharing leads can improve the efficiency of both companies.

Step 2: Qualifying Prospects

Before you go to the time and expense of preparing and delivering a sales presentation to and individual or firm, you should try to learn:

- Whether they have a need for what you offer.
- What role they play in the buying process.
- Whether they have the money to buy.

Basically, qualification is about understanding the situation before you make a sales call. Sales calls, especially in-person sales calls, are expensive. If you have to travel to give a presentation, that effort can represent several hours and hundreds of dollars. You need to evaluate whether or not that call is a good investment for you and your company.

The simplest way to qualify prospects is to ask directly. In general, people with a real need and who have the wherewithal and ability to buy will tell you so. Be careful if someone is evasive or overly vague when you try to pin them down.

It is also important to understand what role the individual plays in the buying process. For example, you certainly want to see qualified decision makers and gatekeepers with the ability to make solid recommendations.

Whether or not you are willing to meet with users, less empowered gatekeepers, or influencers will depend on the size of the opportunity and the costs involved. I once worked with a salesperson who spent almost an entire year meeting with everyone he could who was involved in a particular multimillion-dollar government technology purchase.

Step 3: The Preapproach

This step in the sales process is sometimes called "doing your homework." Before you meet with a prospect, you want to gather as much information as you can about the person and the company you will be seeing.

The research techniques discussed in Chapter 4 are helpful here. If there are any particular questions that I would like answers to before I make a sales call, I often just call my contact and ask. The prospect wants to make the time as productive as you do and will almost always be willing to help you make the best presentation you can.

Step 4: The Sales Presentation

Goals and Objectives

Presentations should meet at least one of the five following goals:

1. Educate the customer.
2. Get the customer's attention.
3. Build interest for the company's products and services.
4. Nurture the customer's desire and conviction.
5. Obtain a customer commitment to action (purchase).

It is not necessary to close the sale on the first presentation. What is important is to recognize that sales presentations, like all other methods of marketing, are an investment and require a fair return on the time, effort, and money spent. When setting goals for a particular presentation, identify all of the value you think you can derive, not just the immediate sale, and work toward ensuring that you get that value.

Unfortunately, many salespeople believe that if they do not close the deal the first time they meet with a prospect, they will never get another chance. As a result, they are willing to potentially damage their long-run prospects for building business if they think it will improve their short-run chances of getting a sale today.

Car dealers can be especially bad at this. I have had salespeople try to take an inordinate amount of my time, pressuring me into making an immediate purchase by running back and forth to their manager, theoretically on my behalf. In the car business, this is sometimes called "the system." Perhaps it worked years ago when it was initially introduced, but today most people I know hate dealing with car dealers, even when they really want the car. Some car companies, such as Saturn and CarMax have done very well by avoiding that whole process.

Stages in the Sales Presentation Process

Approach. The initial part of the presentation should be the easiest. The potential customer is there and willing to listen to what you have to say. All you have to do is talk, ask, and listen yourself.

Unfortunately, a lot of sales are lost in the first minute of the presentation because the salesperson has made a dumb mistake. Some things to remember:

1. *Never make the customer wait*, even if he or she makes you wait. Someone once told me "you are either early or late." Make sure you are early. If you are too early, as will sometimes happen if you travel to a meeting, bring something to work on while you wait.

   Being on time means that you are ready to begin the presentation at the appointed time, not just that you show up. If you need to get your Powerpoint presentation set up or if you have to assemble your demonstration materials, then arrive early enough to do this. It also helps if you let the receptionist of your prospect's assistant know what you need so that they can arrange to have the meeting room available for you to set up.

   On the other hand, if there are circumstances beyond your control (e.g., a cancelled or delayed flight), let your prospect know as soon as possible. In business, everyone is expected to have a cell phone, and prospects are unlikely to accept any excuse for your not letting them know you are going to be late.

   Also, there is always the chance that the prospect might not be able to see you if you must arrive late. It is much better to find that out before you make, or continue to make, a long trip.
2. *Dress appropriately*. A business suit or a coat and tie are almost never wrong. If the prospect is in "business casual," you can just remove your coat.
3. *Turn off or silence all wireless communication devices*. The only exception is if you are establishing communication with your company as part of the presentation.
4. *Avoid being too "chatty."* You are there for a purpose. It is important to be friendly, but sales presentations are not cocktail parties. On the other hand, if the prospect wants to chat, let him or her talk as much as he or she wants provided you still have time for the basics of your presentation. There may be great gems of information in what the prospect is disclosing about himself or herself and the company.

Listening. Here is the secret of a great sales presentation:

If you listen carefully, a qualified buyer will tell you how to sell to them.

In sales, as in life, listening is more important than talking. Most people listen actively only 25 percent of the time. The rest of the time, they are either talking or thinking about what they are going to say next. Active listening requires commitment to focus on the speaker, concentrate on what is being said, and take in nonverbal as well as verbal messages. Research has shown that people who listen more are perceived as not only nicer, but also more interesting. Remember, if you listen, they will tell you what you need to know.

It works like this:

1. Make a key point in your presentation.
2. Notice the response.
3. Ask clarification questions.
4. Listen, listen, listen.
5. Ask more questions to make sure you understand.
6. Listen even more.
7. Change direction if you must, otherwise.
8. Proceed to the next point.

There are several different types of questions that salespeople can ask during presentations. These include data collection, investigation, and validation questions:

Data collection questions are designed to collect needed information that you were not able to obtain during the preapproach stage. In general, you should limit your use of this kind of question in presentation as the prospect may see these questions as indicating a lack of preparation.

If you must ask information questions, you want to make sure that the answer to the question is not readily available elsewhere, like on their Web site. You might also try phrasing the question in a way that indicates that you have done your homework. For example, "I saw in the *Wall Street Journal* that your firm was involved in a new program with the Department of Agriculture. Can you tell me about how that initiative might affect what we can do for you?"

Investigation questions are designed to learn more about the reasons why the prospect is interested in your products and to assess the prospect's current state of mind. The questions we proposed to the plant store in the story at the beginning of the chapter were examples of investigation questions.

Validation questions are used to help get agreement from the prospect. In particular, you use validation questions to:

- Make sure the prospect has understood a point you have made.
- Make sure you understand a point they have made.
- Assess whether the prospect agrees with a point you have made.

Nonverbal communication. Nonverbal communication is the most important element in the communication process. Some researchers claim that less than 10 percent of our personal communication is based on what we say; the rest comes from tone of voice, body posture, and eye movements.

There is some controversy, however, regarding the meaning of specific nonverbal behaviors, in particular body posture. There are a lot of books and training programs out there that will tell you, for example, that people who have their arms crossed in front of their chest is communicating that they are closed and resistant to what you are saying. Other researchers (you may want to investigate the work done in Neuro-Linguistic Programming or NLP) argue that the same gestures could simply indicate that the person was cold or just more comfortable sitting that way. The point here is that when reading another person's body language it is important to be open to alternative interpretations.

In regards to you own body language, the key is honesty. If you assume that whatever you are thinking is coming out through your body language, you will be more careful about what you are thinking in the presence of prospects. And, if you are careful about what you are thinking, you will not have to worry about your body language.

Sales Presentation Strategies

There are four basic kinds of presentation strategies you could consider. Understand hat one is not better than the others. They are just alternatives that you can use based on the specific circumstances you may be in.

Memorized presentations. Memorized presentations are the easiest presentations to learn and to give. The salesperson talks about 90 percent of the time, following a (hopefully) carefully prepared script. Memorized presentations are good for:

- New salespeople who cannot yet manage a presentation on their own.
- Ensuring consistent delivery of critical information with maximum efficiency.
- Making sure that the salesperson follows through to the close.

On the downside, memorized presentations may:

- Discuss some areas not important to the individual prospect and leave out some that are.
- Reduce the importance of the salesperson making it more difficult for her to establish the trusted advisor relationship with the prospect.
- Tend to seem high pressure.
- Fall apart if the salesperson gets distracted from the script.

Multimedia presentations. With the availability of powerful and inexpensive hardware and presentation software, multimedia PowerPoint presentations have become extremely popular with salespeople. They can be interesting, entertaining, and powerful. Products can be shown in use; customers can give taped testimonials; and graphics can be used to explain technical details.

Although multimedia presentations can be very effective when used properly, they are, at their heart, just memorized presentations presented in more effective and entertaining ways. Like memorized presentations, multimedia presentations:

- Are likely to cover some issues that are not of concern to the prospect, while missing others.
- Can reduce the importance of the role of the salesperson, making it more difficult for him/her to establish rapport.
- Are difficult to interrupt to address immediate questions that the prospect might have.

Need satisfaction presentations. The needs satisfaction presentation follows a specific, three-step format:

- Need identification stage: questioning the customer to discover needs.
- Need analysis stage: by combining knowledge of the company's products and services with the recognition of the customer's needs, determining how to best meet those needs.
- Need satisfaction stage: presenting the company's solution to the customer's needs.

This is a good format to use for midrange products where the price does not justify the investment of more than one sales call. In this case, the prospect and the salesperson basically follow the buyer decision model from beginning to end.

Problem-solving presentations. Problem-solving presentations, also known a "consultative selling," involve the salesperson facilitating the prospect in developing a solution to the prospect's problem. In other words, the salesperson acts as a consultant to the prospect, putting the resources of that salesperson's company on display in the development of the solution.

In this type of presentation, it is specifically the goal of the salesperson to become the trusted advisor to the prospect, and all activities are geared toward earning and keeping that trust.

As such, these types of presentations tend to be far more customized and less structured than the other types of presentations discussed. In fact, the "presentation" may extend over several meetings as the prospect outlines needs, and the salesperson goes back to develop solutions.

This type of presentation is best when attempting to build long-term relationships with key customers or partners in our external environment. Stakes will be high for buyer and seller, and it will be important for each of you to be confident that the relationship will be mutually beneficial.

Step 5: Negotiation and Clarification

Negotiation Guidelines

Nothing seems to ruin relationships more than disappointed expectations. You think something is supposed to happen or that the other person should behave in a certain way. When they don't, you feel let down, even betrayed. And, because lack of clarity usually works both ways, the other person is apt to feel the same way, making resolution of the situation even more difficult.

In business, marketing and sales must accept responsibility for setting and clarifying these expectations. Customers need to know, prior to the sale, that the organization will make good on the claims made in its advertisements and by its salespeople. Negative "surprises," even small ones, during the sales or delivery process can destroy a salesperson's or an entire organization's credibility with a customer.

It is critical, therefore, for marketers and salespeople to make sure that the organization and its customers have equally clear and identical ideas about what is to be delivered, at what price, under what circumstances, and what remedies will be taken on either side if there is a problem.

Unfortunately, many organizations hide these responsibilities behind complicated legal contracts and "agreements" that require an experienced attorney, with a magnifying glass, to decipher. The key to clarity is simplicity, rather than exhaustive elaboration of contingencies. Each step in the sales process, from the first contact the customer makes with the organization to the last time the customer experiences a problem, should be crystal clear to customer and provider. In that way, inaccurate/unrealistic assumptions, and the resultant potential for disappointment and hard feelings is minimized.

The win–win concept. "Win–win" is one of those phrases that seems to have lost a lot of its meaning through overuse. At its core, it means that, in dealing with your company, customers have to believe that you have their best interest at heart as well as your own. This is the essence of the trusted advisor role. If you want the big success, your customers have to trust you. Even if it is against your own interests in the short term, a win–win approach will most certainly pay off in the long term.

However, win–win is no longer just a soft, nice-to-do kind of approach. It is essential. In today's highly communicated world, word that you are untrustworthy will get out and can haunt you long after that sale is over and with people you may never get a chance to meet as a result.

Basic ground rules. Here are some basic ground rules for successful negotiation:

- Be clear about what you want and why you want it.
- Don't ever say something that is not the truth.

- Stay calm and focused on the key issues. Don't lose sight of what's important.
- Stay on your message. Continue to reinforce and support your value proposition.
- Never be negative. Not about your competitors, not about yourself or your organization, and certainly not about the customer or their organizations. Not about people or politics, or the weather, or anything!
- Leave your ego at home. You can kill the deal and the relationship by trying to show off or be "right" about something.
- Never resurrect dead issues.
- Know when to walk. Negotiators have a term called "best alternative to a negotiated agreement" (BATNA). If it is clear to you that the deal the customer wants would not be a win–win, don't do it. Even if you get the sale, it will come back to bite you later.

Customer Objections

After the presentation is over, or even during the presentation, the prospect is likely to raise some questions, issues, or objections related to buying your product or service. If you are to make a sale, you must be able to understand and deal effectively with the objections that prospects raise.

The clarification step is sometimes referred to as "overcoming objections." I do not like that term. It implies that there is some kind of war going on in which the salesperson must prevail. If you are thinking like that, you might want to consider another career. In today's business environment, only win–win relationships work over the long run.

Types of objections. There are three types of objections that a prospect might raise:

1. *Considerations:* Considerations are legitimate reasons why your product or service might not work for them. These are the non-negotiable evaluative criteria we discussed in the buyer decision model.

   For example, if someone tried to sell me a software package that was incompatible with the operating system on my laptop computer, it probably would not matter how effective that software was. I cannot use it, unless it is so powerful that it would be worth my changing my operating system or even buying a new computer just to use that software.

   Considerations are potential deal breakers and must be identified and treated as such. If it is clear that the particular issue the prospect has is not something that you and your company can manage, then simply say so. You may then either leave or, if appropriate, provide whatever other assistance or information you can to that prospect. I have had such prospects turn into good referral sources for me, even though they never bought anything from me.
2. *Hidden questions:* Sometimes a prospect will couch a question as an objection. For example, the objection "I don't like that color" can be seen as really asking "What other colors does it come in?"

Whenever possible, try to reframe each objection as a hidden question and a request for more information.

3. *A dishonest no:* Many people do not want to come out and just say "no," especially if they like you. Instead, they will continue to raise objections in the hope that you will give up and not make them at fault for the failure of the sale.

After a little while, it is fairly easy to tell if the prospect is raising legitimate objections or if they are just hunting around for a polite way to say no. I have found that the best way to handle this situation is to be direct. Most people will appreciate your candor and your concern for their feelings.

Dealing with objections. The sales literature suggests many ways of dealing with customer objections. I have found the following few suggestions to be helpful to me.

1. *Turn it around*: Turn the prospect's objection into a question of your own. This gets the prospect thinking in new, more positive ways. For example:

Prospect: I like the product, but it is too big.
Salesperson: Can you tell me more about your size requirements?

2. *Direct denial*: Sometimes you might need to use a confrontational, but polite, strategy for dealing with an objection that is based on a false or damaging assumption. It is never a good idea to let such an assumption go unchallenged. The fact that you said nothing could be taken as validation of it. Tread lightly, though. As we have said several times, people do not like to be made wrong. For example:

Prospect: I was told recently that you had to recall all of your production for the last two months because of a faulty relay in your switch mechanism.
Salesperson: I'm not sure where you could have heard that. We have not had a recall on any of our products for over 10 years. If you like, I can provide the data for you. Your source was mistaken.

3. *Compensating for deficiencies:* This technique moves the prospect from focusing on a feature your product performs poorly to one in which it excels. The new feature must be important to the customer, however. For example:

Prospect: The response time on your product is too slow. Your competition's response time is two-tenths of a second faster.
Salesperson: I agree with you. My product is two-tenths of a second slower. However, please note that it also costs 25 percent less per unit and has 10 percent fewer returns.

4. *Third-party endorsements*: In this technique, the salesperson uses specific outside parties to bolster arguments in the presentation. Because the references are specific, this technique can add credibility to the presentation. For example:

Prospect: Your customer service has been questionable, and it is important I have tech support 24/7.

Salesperson: I agree with you that our customer service was not what it should be several years ago. However, we made the investment to improve customer service, and now it is among the best in the industry. Gracie Electronics felt as you did but was willing to try us and is now one of our best customers.

5. *Defer:* This technique is most commonly used when the customer raises a concern about price early in the presentation before the value proposition has been clearly defined. Example:

Prospect: (before the full value of the product has been explained): What is the cost of your product?

Salesperson: I can appreciate your interest in knowing the price of the product, but I would ask you to hold off just a minute until I know a little more about your product requirements.

6. *Trial offer*: A trial offer is one of the best strategies to calm a prospect's objections. Although it does not take the place of a good sales presentation, it does allow the prospect to go straight to the experience step of the decision process. In addition, it adds credibility to your claims about product suitability because you are willing to let the prospect try before they buy.

Two things are necessary for a successful trial:

- The terms of the trial offer (time period, responsibility for damage, etc.) must be defined beforehand.
- If use of the product involves some level of training or technical expertise, the prospect needs to be fully checked out before the product is left with them.

Trial Offer—Example

Prospect: I'm not willing to make a commitment to your copier today. It seems complicated and hard to use.

Salesperson: I can appreciate your concerns. How about I have our service department install one for you and let you try it for one week. I will come by and demonstrate it for you.

It must be made clear that these are certainly not the only ways for salespeople to handle customer objections, issues, or concerns. They are meant to be illustrative of the many ways available to salespeople to treat customer concerns with respect and, at the same time, move the sales process toward a win–win conclusion.

Step 6: Closing

Many salespeople fail because they do not ask for the order. Remember that if you have done your job and get to this point, the prospect wants to buy. The next part of your job is to help that prospect to do it.

Again, the direct way is the simplest and usually the best. Often a simple question such as "Do I have your approval to proceed?" or "Is there anything else you need to clarify before I place the order?" are all that is needed.

There are a lot of sales trainers that offer a lot of different "manipulative" techniques for getting people to agree to a sale. I tend to avoid any kind of behavior that has even a hint of dishonesty to it. If you have been successful at achieving trusted advisor status to this point, it would be a shame to waste it at the last moment.

There are three fundamental steps to closing:

1. Ask for the order.
2. Be patient.
3. Stop trying to sell.

If you have successfully brought the prospect through the buyer decision process up to the decision making step, you have done your job. Prospects must now be given the time and "space" necessary for them to make their own decision their own way. Anything else simply interrupts that process. Have confidence. If you have done the sales job honestly and with sincere concern for the overall welfare of the prospect, that is all you can do.

In particular, don't lose patience and try to restart the selling process. This is called "selling past the close." It almost never works and is much more likely to derail the whole process.

The Clarification—Closing Cycle

When you attempt to close, you will get one of three possible responses:

1. Yes
2. No
3. Objection.

If they say yes, great! Stop selling and move on to making sure that you and your company keep your agreements.

If they say no, all is not lost. Try to find out why. If the "no" is based on some hidden objection that you might clarify cycle back to the clarification step and see what you can do to move the sale forward again. However, if the person's ''no'' is real and he or she has made up his or her mind not to buy from you, do not try to push past this. The chances of your getting anywhere are very small. Besides, just because people do not buy from you this time does not mean that you in any way want to damage the chances of them buying from you another time. Express your thanks for their time and your respect for their judgment and let them know that you are still there to assist them if the selection they have made does not work out.

If they raise another objection, just go back to the clarification stage, work it out with them, and try to close gain.

Step 7: Delivery and Follow-up

Here is an old saying in sales: ''The deal is not closed until the check clears.'' Even if you have agreement in the sales interaction, it is always possible for the buyer to back out.

Professional salespeople take their relationships with customers personally. The sale was closed on their word, their promises. It is up to the salespeople to ensure that those promises are kept and customers get what they think they paid for.

In this context:

- Make sure that the people in your own company responsible for delivery deliver exactly what was ordered, exactly when it was promised.
- If there is any problem with delivery, call the customer yourself and work things out. Business is always personal. To that customer, you are your company, not someone from shipping they have never heard of.
- Always send handwritten thank-you notes. Almost everyone appreciates them, and almost no one sends them.
- Call the customer soon after the order has been delivered to make sure that everything is alright. Then call them again in a month or so to make sure again.
- Don't forget to ask for referrals from happy customers. It's very beneficial to you and, interestingly enough, commits them more firmly to being happy with you.

SUMMARY

☑ The decision space is that place in the prospect's mind where the decision to buy or not buy is made.
☑ Salespeople need to become trusted advisors to the prospective buyer.
☑ Prospecting is the identification of potential buyers.
☑ Effective sales presentations are conversations between the prospect and the salesperson, where the salesperson tries to clarify the prospect's needs and provide solutions to them.

- ☑ The key to effective sales presentations is listening, not talking.
- ☑ The key to successful sales is an insistence on a "win–win" result for all parties.
- ☑ The key to successful negotiating is clarity and honesty.
- ☑ Most customer objections are really requests for additional information.

14

Standing by Your Word

This chapter is intended to be short and sweet. I discuss the importance of keeping agreements and business ethics in the strategic marketing process.

KEEPING AGREEMENTS AND BUSINESS ETHICS

Ethics work. If an organization states clearly what it is going to do, ensures that the customer understands, and then just does it, that organization will greatly minimize customer problems and greatly facilitate the personal trust that maintains long-term customer relationships. Your marketing efforts are useless without a trustworthy organization behind them. There are many reasons to strive toward ethical behavior.

Ethics Are Practical

Ethics are not only "right," they are the only practical way to do business.

Protect Your Reputation

Ethical companies also develop a good reputation. I think everyone has at least one story of a situation where a company went out of its way to "do the right thing." On the other hand, we all have stories where a company did something we considered to be morally or ethically wrong. And we tell those stories to other people, sometimes for years!

In today's Internet society, there are any places where people can go to complain. It is almost impossible to "keep things quiet," as many politicians and corporations have learned.

Avoid Expense

Ethics are also less expensive.

In most cases, the cost of handling a problem after the fact is much greater than the cost of preventing it in the first place. This is especially the case if the problem gets to the litigation stage. People rarely sue as a first choice. They generally sue when they feel that there is no other avenue to resolve the difficulty. And, whatever side you are on and whether or not you are in the right, lawyers are expensive. Everyone (except the lawyers) ends up losing.

Feel Good about Yourself and Your Company

The most important reason for ethics is inside of yourself. You know what the right thing to do is in almost every situation. When you do the right thing, people know. It becomes pure pleasure to deal with them, and they enjoy dealing with you. You spend so much of your life building your business. Enjoy it!

SUMMARY

- ☑ Ethics are morally right.
- ☑ Ethics work.

15

Calling in the Pros

There is a profound difference between understanding how a process works and being able to effectively design and implement each part of its execution. This chapter is designed to assist you in deciding when and how to use marketing professionals and other types of consultants in the planning and implementation phases of a marketing program.

KNOWING WHEN AND HOW TO GET HELP

There are several reasons why you might want to seek a marketing consultant:

- Professional support can provide you some significant benefits that you will have to weigh against the investment that is required.
- Professionals bring in experience and "lessons learned" from many other situations with many other clients. Some of these lessons you may have to learn for yourself, at your own expense.
- Professionals may have expertise and experience in core operational areas that you do not have time to develop. These areas may include market research, graphic arts, and media buying.
- Professionals provide a "sounding board" that allows you to discuss core business issues with an impartial, expert outsider who may help you identify inaccuracies in your assumptions about your business, market, and business environment.
- Because they have experience and expertise in certain marketing areas, professional may actually be able to do a job for you faster and less expensively that you could do it for yourself.

There are some downsides, however:

- Unless you are using one of the services mentioned below, good professionals do not come cheap.
- Although experience is certainly valuable, in some cases, professionals may be inclined to offer you the same "solution" that worked for

another client they had. Be especially wary of consultants who are specific to your industry. This tendency to try to do what worked before can be dangerous because every marketing situation is different.

PROFESSIONAL SUPPORT OPTIONS

As an entrepreneur, you have three basic options when it comes to using outside help. The first is not to use outside help at all. This is probably the best option for you if:

- You are already an expert in marketing.
- You do not have any extra money to invest in outside help.
- Your marketing issues are straightforward and do not require outside expertise.

If you select this option and do your marketing program yourself, I strongly recommend that you still get a trusted friend or associate involved in the process. You need to have someone, preferably independent of you, who can ask you the tough questions and challenge your shaky assumptions.

Outsource the Marketing Process Entirely

One very tempting option for the entrepreneur who is unsure of himself or herself and has funds to invest is to outsource the marketing function entirely. There are a lot of consulting firms and advertising agencies out there that will help you do that.

In general, I do not recommend that entrepreneurs outsource their marketing efforts entirely. This is because:

- It is very expensive to have outsiders do everything for you. Most of these firms either bill you an hourly rate or compute their fixed price contract based on an hourly rate. They will charge for all of the time that they have to spend learning about your business, your market, and your competitors. Good marketing firms are very motivated to do an outstanding job for you, but it will cost.
- You lose control of the process. Although it is tempting to expect that you will stay involved at every step, my experience has shown that clients will tend to cede more and more control over time, especially if the firm is getting good results.
- No marketing firm will have the understanding, experience, insight, and operational knowledge that you have.
- Many marketing firms and most advertising agencies receive either commissions or markups from subcontractors and media outlets that they utilize on your behalf. In this system, the more of your money they spend, the more money they make. There is little incentive to keep costs down.

Consultants and Coaches

As an option to using a full-service advertising agency or marketing firm, you can retain one of the many excellent marketing consultants or business coaches that practice in almost every city. These consultants and coaches work with entrepreneurs to help them do the marketing job themselves.

The major difference between consultants and coaches is that consultants tend to be experts in operational areas, such as market research, whereas coaches are experts at facilitating the client's efforts and may not know much about any particular operational area.

The good news for the small business entrepreneur is that sometimes expert help is available at little or no cost through a number of government and volunteer agencies. These include:

- Service Corps of Retired Executives (SCORE) www.score.org
- Small Business Administration www.sba.gov
- Small Business Development Centers: These are a program of the Small Business Administration and are housed in various colleges and universities around the country. http://www.sba.gov/aboutsba/sbaprograms/sbdc/index.html
- Kutztown University Small Business Development Center: I mention this one in particular because of their extensive catalog of free, online courses. http://www.kutztownsbdc.org
- Chambers of Commerce: the site for the U.S. Chamber of Commerce has a directory where you can easily find Chambers of Commerce in your local area www.chamberofcommerce.com
- Economic Development Offices of local governments
- Local colleges and universities: The business schools at local colleges and universities are often seeking real businesses for their students to help. The businesses get free assistance and the students get invaluable experience. I have helped over 400 companies in my career through various student projects

Implementation Subcontractors

A third option is to plan and manage the marketing function yourself and use subcontractors to do the specific parts of the marketing program that require particular expertise. These areas of expertise can include:

- Market research
- Graphics
- Mailings
- Copy writing
- Public relations
- Media buying

Almost any metropolitan area or small city has several of these. (The county of 400,000 people where I currently live has 43 marketing and advertising firms and consultants listed in the Yellow Pages.)

Although I usually do not recommend that entrepreneurs engage full-service agencies, using experts in specific operational areas often is a good idea. They can get the job done quickly and, frequently, at lower cost than you can.

Cautions in Using Outside Help

As an entrepreneur, marketing needs to become a core competency of yours, if is not already. If you need to work with an outside consultant or firm, make sure that you can understand and be involved at every step of the process. Be wary of anyone who has a "proprietary" process that produces results or recommendations, if that process is never clearly disclosed to you. Ninety-five percent of marketing is applied, disciplined, common sense. It does not require any "smoke and mirrors."

Make sure you have an airtight nondisclosure agreement if you have any proprietary business information or intellectual capital you want to protect. Consultants work with other firms and may be in a position to disclose private information about you. Although most business consultants, at least the ones I have known over the last thirty years, are highly ethical people, it does not hurt to protect yourself, even if you only spell out what you do and do not consider to be private. Also, make sure that your agreement specifies that you have exclusive ownership of all work products.

Pricing for consultants is of two types: firm fixed price and hourly.

- Firm fixed-price agreements need to spell out exactly the scope of work the consultant will perform and when the work is due. It should also spell out what procedures will be followed to expand that scope of work should it be required to do so.
- Hourly rates should include incidental expenses. It's generally better to pay a slightly higher hourly rate than to be "nickeled and dimed" for local travel, phone calls, and photocopying. Besides, you want the consultant working, not tracking small expenses. Agreements should always have a "not-to-exceed" number of hours to accomplish the tasks specified in the scope of work. Although you run the risk of the consultant working the maximum hours allowed, that is a much smaller risk than having the individual bill you if he or she runs over.

SUMMARY

☑ Professionals should be used, but used sparingly and carefully.
☑ Make sure all agreements are clear.
☑ Make sure your intellectual property is protected.
☑ Always maintain control of your own marketing.

16

Conclusion

I want to make a few things clear here at the end of this book.

NO ANALYSIS PARALYSIS

First, I am not trying to get you to analyze your business to death. I, too, am an entrepreneur and have a "ready, fire, aim" attitude toward trying things out and getting things done. I have little patience for the "paralysis by analysis" that I see in so many companies.

What I have tried to do is provide you a complete box of powerful conceptual and analytical tools that you can use if and whenever you need them.

I would suggest that, at a minimum, you go though the following:

1. *Goal setting:* to clarify you personal and professional objectives
2. *SWOT:* so that you take some time to consider your entire business environment
3. *555 Matrix:* to help you asses what makes you special and how you could become even more special
4. *BCG matrix:* (If you have multiple products) to help you balance new products with established products

ENTREPRENEURS ARE "I" PEOPLE

Entrepreneurs are special people. You are what makes business the intensely fascinating process that it is. A close associate of mine (my wife Jan, actually) refers to the "5 Is" of the entrepreneur:

- Intuition
- Inspiration
- Insight
- Initiative
- In-depth knowledge

These are talents and, like musical talent or athletic talent, the possessors of these talents must develop them. This requires and disciplined commitment to doing all you can to employ your considerable talents to make your business work.

One of the main purposes of this book is to provide you with some "exercises" to help you develop your business acumen and to teach you to maintain a big picture orientation, even if you currently have a very small business. Remember that many of today's biggest successes started their businesses with almost nothing but a dream. The difference between the successes and the rest is that the successes:

- Had the willingness to look past the conventional business wisdom of their time and see the opportunities waiting for them in the future,
- Had the discipline and determination to carry out their plans despite the many naysayers they met along the way, and (mostly)
- Had the ability to find personal joy and satisfaction in providing significant value to others.

I hope I have provided you a bit of help in your entrepreneurial journey.

SUMMARY

☑ Avoid "analysis paralysis."
☑ Entrepreneurs are "I" people.
☑ Marketing should flow smoothly and easily.

Index

About the Author

ROBERT F. EVERETT, Ph.D., teaches marketing at Kutztown University in Pennsylvania. He has also taught at the Johns Hopkins University and the University of Maryland, College Park. Besides working as an independent business consultant, Dr. Everett has been Regional Director for the American Management Association, Vice President at software developer The Orcutt Group, Director of Business Development for the high-tech consultancy Selbre Associates, and a principal in an advertising agency.